WITHDRAWN

LUNCH HOUR

LUNCH HOUR

Jean Kerr

Doubleday & Company, Inc., Garden City, New York
1982

Library of Congress Cataloging in Publication Data

Kerr, Jean.
Lunch hour.

I. Title.
PS3521.E744L8 1982   812'.54   AACR2
ISBN: 0-385-17646-5
Library of Congress Catalog Card Number: 81-43601

A portion of this work appeared in BEST PLAYS of 1980–1981, edited by Otis L. Guernsey, Jr., published by Dodd, Mead & Company, Inc.

for Janet and Don

LUNCH HOUR

LUNCH HOUR was first presented by Robert Whitehead and Roger L. Stevens at the Ethel Barrymore Theater, in New York City, on November 12, 1980. It was directed on Broadway by Mike Nichols; the scenery was designed by Oliver Smith, the costumes by Ann Roth, and the lighting by Jennifer Tipton. The cast, in the order of appearance, was as follows:

Oliver .... Sam Waterston

Nora .... Susan Kellermann

Carrie .... Gilda Radner

Leo .... Max Wright

Peter .... David Rasche

Scene is the interior of a beach house in the Bridgehampton area of Long Island.

CHARACTERS

OLIVER DeVRECK, in his mid-thirties, attractive rather than handsome. Since he is really on the thin side, it is surprising to learn that he's on a diet. Casually, though not sloppily, dressed.

NORA DeVRECK, his wife, in her early thirties, beautiful and impeccably dressed.

CARRIE SACHS is twenty-three, slender, and very pretty. The dress she is wearing when she appears is not unbecoming, but it seems in some way prim, a trace old-fashioned. Though she is married, her effect is that of an appealing but not quite organized teenager.

LEO SIMPSON is an actor in his early thirties. His clothes are casual but carefully chosen and rather raffish, as he is.

PETER SACHS is fortyish, looks and dresses like the very rich sportsman and art dealer he is; he tends to compensate for a mild, secret insecurity by being a little patronizing and rather more dashingly romantic than he actually feels.

SETTING

A beach house in the Hamptons, built into a hilltop on the bay side. There would be a long, steep walk down to the beach. Through the sliding glass panels in the rear wall that lead out onto the sun deck, we can see the tops of trees, mostly pines. On the deck we can see the beginning of a stairwell that leads to a basement apartment, built into the hillside just below, and then winds down to the beach. Tiger lilies grow wild here. Alongside the sliding glass doors—these are usually wide open—are wall curtains, one of which covers the switches that operate the deck lights and the amplification system for music when wanted.

The front door, which is the main entrance from the road, is at extreme stage Left. Downstage Right, there is a small section of counter to separate the living and dining areas from the kitchen. In front of the counter is a small, two-person settee. Near it is an end table. Upstage Right there are arches opening toward bedrooms and bathroom. A slightly elevated section of the room is given over to OLIVER's desk; directly below the desk stands a lighted fish tank. The elevated segment is reached by two stairs above the counter, and continues toward the deck area, running behind the long sofa in the very center of the room. The elevated level is easily approachable from either end.

There are quite a few plants in unusual containers scattered about the room, though not overwhelmingly and not for comic effect. We only become aware of how many there are when they're talked about. The furnishings generally are not beach-house-sloppy: no modern furniture, no rush rugs, no canvas. The room has been lovingly decorated by an actor with some taste. Bar shelving is built into the front of the counter. Up on the level, against the back wall that contains the switches, stands another small end table, with a cowbell on it. The room is comfortable and spacious enough to take care of its own clutter, and the fact that occasionally the breeze from the deck makes the wall curtains billow out pleasantly adds to the sense of spaciousness and freedom.

THE TIME

The last day of June, a Saturday

ACT ONE—Early afternoon

ACT TWO, Scene One—Late afternoon to early evening

ACT TWO, Scene Two—After dark

ACT ONE

OLIVER *is at his desk, working on the long, slithering galley proofs of his new book.* NORA *enters, preparing to leave. She is smartly dressed in summer clothes and carries a straw basket.*

NORA

Honey, how can you stand all this sun?

OLIVER
(Continues working)
That's why we came out here—to get all this sun. I'll be golden brown, like a waffle.

NORA

You'll be blind. It's right in your eye.
(Picks up a pair of very lightly tinted sunglasses and puts them on him)
Better?

OLIVER

Yeah, I guess it is—

NORA
(Kissing him lightly on the top of his head)
Of course it is. I'm always right. That's why you married me.

OLIVER

That was not the reason.

NORA

You still haven't had your lunch. I put the hard-boiled eggs and the tuna in the icebox.

OLIVER

Did you—

NORA

(*Before* he *can say it*)

Yes, I did rinse the oil out of the tuna fish. I don't know why you're on this crazy diet. You're not overweight.

OLIVER

(*Continues to work*)

None of my suits fit.

NORA

You should really get some new clothes. All your suits look like you ordered them from an L. L. Bean catalogue.

OLIVER

I like them. Anyway, I don't have time to buy new ones. I just need to lose four pounds.

NORA

You could stop eating M&M's at the movies.

OLIVER

Never.

(9)

NORA

The other night, you ate three of those great big bags—

OLIVER

But that was a *very* bad movie.

NORA
(*A little testiness coming through*)

You picked it.

OLIVER

Yes, and I was warned. It said, right in the reviews, "Powerful—but not for the squeamish." When will I learn? I am the squeamish.

(*Phone rings*)

Get that, and remember—

NORA

I remember. You're out. And how long are you going to *be* out?

OLIVER

All day. All night. Look, just say I'm not here this weekend—

NORA

You're so firm. And so lacking in curiosity.
(*Into the phone*)

Hello. Yes, this is Mrs. DeVreck. No, I'm sorry, he's not here. No, actually I'm not expecting him. He's staying in the city this weekend. Is there any kind of an emergency? I could give you the number there. Well, certainly. That'll be fine. And who shall I say called? *Who?* That's all right, it's no bother. 'Bye.
(*To* OLIVER, *as* she *hangs up*)

Obviously, one of your ladies. She sounded very tense.

OLIVER
(*A trace of exasperation*)

They are not my ladies, they are my patients. And why on earth would you offer to give her the New York number? She'd just get the answering service.

NORA

Because I wanted to sound lovable and cooperative. Not jealous and suspicious.

OLIVER

You're jealous because I am well known to be catnip. When I go to a hotel, teenagers hide in my closets. Movie actresses proposition me. But why are you suspicious?

NORA

Because she said she was Mrs. Amagansett.

OLIVER

And?

NORA

You know there is nowhere, anywhere, a Mrs. Amagansett. There are *no* Amagansetts.

OLIVER

Wasn't there an Indian tribe?

NORA

I don't know about Indians, but I can tell you that this woman just didn't want to give her real name.

OLIVER
(*Finally looking up from his work*)

And you conclude that . . . ?

NORA

I don't conclude, I never conclude. I'm over all that.

OLIVER

You're over it? What have you got to be over?

NORA

Let's not, okay? Let's just not. But I do have one question. How come you won't answer the phone?

OLIVER

(*Back to work*)

But you know how come.

NORA

I know you're trying to finish that book. But then, you've been trying to finish it for eighteen months. That never kept your great heart from caring about the poor, the huddled masses, the beautiful women—

OLIVER

Oh, my God, Nora!

NORA

I'm sorry. Erase that, I never said it. I never thought it.

OLIVER

But you did say it—

NORA

Well, there you are. A little flare-up of my old paranoia. It's like bursitis. You think you're over it and then suddenly you start getting these damn little twitches. Now, you were saying. . . .

OLIVER

I don't know what the hell I was saying. I don't know what I'm thinking. Actually, the list of things I don't know is getting longer and kind of out of hand.

NORA

Don't churn. You won't get anything done. You'll start smoking again. You'll hate yourself.

(He *remains silent*)

Come on, Oliver. I'm declaring a cease-fire.

OLIVER

Okay, okay. . . .

NORA

Anyway, what's so sacred and so special about this weekend?

OLIVER

Tomorrow will be July one. And if I don't get these proofs back to Doubleday—

NORA

(*Exasperated*)

What's the rush?

OLIVER

(*In the same rhythm*)

I promised!

NORA

(*Staring at him, then speaking suddenly*)

Honey, look! Look out there!

(*Points to the view through the sliding glass doors*)

OLIVER

Why? What's *out* there?

NORA

What's out there? The water's out there.

OLIVER

I knew that. I didn't think it moved.

NORA

But look at it today! It's so postcard-beautiful. Why don't you forget about the galleys for an hour. Go swimming.

OLIVER

Honey, I can't. You know I can't.

NORA

Oliver, why don't you surprise me just once and do something on the spur of the moment? Spontaneously!

OLIVER

As soon as I'm through with this book.

NORA

Why do we rent a beach house? You never go in the water.

OLIVER

Sure I do.

NORA
(*Shaking her head hopelessly*)

Uh-uh, never.
(*Starting for the front door*)

I've got to go. If I'm late, mother punishes me by talking about what she wants sung at her funeral.

OLIVER

Her funeral? Yesterday I saw her jogging.

NORA

That's right. She jogs every day.

OLIVER
(*Teasing*)

Are you afraid of your mother?

NORA

Don't be silly. I'm a mature, intelligent woman. Of course I'm afraid of my mother.
(*At the door, beach bag over her arm*)
But she means well, and she loves *you*.

OLIVER

I know she does and I love her.
(*Just as casually, almost experimentally*)
I love you.

NORA
(*Slight pause, and not so casually*)

Do you?
(*Quickly*)
Don't answer. You can take the afternoon to mull that over.
(*Halfway out the door*)
Hey, I'm taking the car. You won't need it, will you?

OLIVER

No, but wouldn't it be quicker to walk over the dune to your mother's place?

NORA

Much quicker, but you get your shoes full of sand. Anyway, I want to go to the Deli later.

(She's gone)

OLIVER
(Calling after the closed door)

'Bye! Check the mailbox!

(Phone on his desk rings)

I will ignore that and it will go away. It will stop. Okay, I'll just turn the damn thing off.

(He presses the button that turns his desk phone off, but we can hear the phone in the bedroom still ringing. OLIVER gets up, with a sigh, and starts toward the bedroom as though to turn that one off too, then gives up and heads back to his desk. Turns his phone on again; it rings and he picks it up)

Hel-LO! Oh, Alex. You didn't drag me from anywhere. I'm right here beside the phone. Because I didn't want to pick it up. You're right. I'm in a charming mood. Look, I know the book is due on Friday. You'll get it on Friday. Then, what did you call about? I sent you four titles. Well, I'm sorry the salesmen don't like any of them. Let them think of a new one. Oh, you've got one. Let's hear it. Whose Life Is It Anyway? Oh, my God, Alex, that's already been used. What? Oh, I see. Whose Wife Is It Anyway. Alex, lie down, you're tired.

(Front doorbell rings)

Alex, there's somebody at the door. I will find out when I go to the door. Yeah, I'll think about it. Sure, sure, I'll sleep on it. Alex, I have got to stop this damn doorbell! Okay.

(OLIVER hangs up abruptly and darts to the front door, opening it to CARRIE SACHS. CARRIE is pretty and seems

*somewhat fussed to see him. She is slender and her
clothes are well made but somehow less than chic)*

CARRIE

You Dr. DeVreck?

OLIVER

That's right.

CARRIE

But you're not here. You're not coming for the whole weekend.
(She *crosses to center, surveying the place)*

OLIVER

But I am here and what can I do for you? Oh, just a minute. You
are Mrs. Amagansett.

CARRIE

Mrs. Who? Oh, yes. Wasn't that a dumb name to pick? But I
didn't think she'd ask my name and all of a sudden I couldn't
think of any name at all. Not even Jones or Smith or Harris.
Amagansett is where I live. 9 Dunes Mere Road, Amagansett!

OLIVER

Fine. Now we've got your number, what's your name?

CARRIE

Look, I don't want to make up another name—

OLIVER

No, don't. I don't think you've got the hang of it.

CARRIE

See, I'd rather not give you my real name—

OLIVER

Then, don't. Do you want to state your business? If you're checking on the house, we're renting it through Labor Day.

CARRIE

No, it's not the house. You mean you rent it?
(*Touring the room*)
I'd never rent a place with this many of somebody else's plants. I'd worry that they'd die. I'd lie awake nights. You mean she's gone? But that's not possible. I just talked to her one minute—two minutes—ago. And I let my cab go. Oh, dear. And I thought I was handling this so well.

OLIVER

Do I gather that it is my wife you wish to see?

CARRIE

Yes, but I gather she's gone. And probably for the whole weekend, too. Why are people so devious?

OLIVER

That's such a good question, I'll ask you. Why are you so devious? What do you want? *Who* do you want?

CARRIE

I wanted to talk to your wife. But I wanted to talk to her alone. And now I'm stranded here.
(*Heading toward his desk*)
Could I possibly use your phone and call a cab to pick me up here?

OLIVER

Well, of course you can. But there are only two cabs and at this hour they'd be at the station. There could be quite a delay.

CARRIE

Look, if I could just call the cab I could sit outside on the deck and wait for it. You look busy, or you look like you'd like to look busy.

OLIVER

That's all right. I'll call.
> (*Goes to his desk and dials, glances at* CARRIE *as he waits for an answer*)

Hello, Eddie. This is Dr. DeVreck, on Valley Road. Can I get a cab here? There's a lady who's going to—
> (*To* CARRIE)

Where are you going to?

CARRIE

I'll figure that out.

OLIVER
> (*Into phone*)

She'll tell you. Okay, but do what you can to hurry it up. Okay, thank you.
> (*Hangs up*)

CARRIE
> (*Edging toward the deck doors*)

I'll sit out here and be out of your way.

OLIVER

If you're sure you don't mind. Listen, it's hot out there. Would you like a drink?

CARRIE

Oh, dear no. Never. Oh, yeah, I'd have a glass of water.

OLIVER

Water? Just plain water?
(He's *getting it from a pitcher on the bar*)

CARRIE

I'll tell you what. I'd take two glasses of water.

OLIVER

I can get you a pitcher of water.

CARRIE

No, two glasses are enough. For now.

OLIVER

Want something to read? We're through with the paper.

CARRIE
(*Putting down the large bag* she *carries*)
I have the paper. It's in here. I *think* it's in here.
(*In her efforts to find it, she fishes out eyeglasses, several small zippered cosmetic bags, a purse, a bottle of suntan lotion, two bathing suits, a towel, a hairbrush, and other assorted items, depositing them temporarily on the chaise longue near her on the deck*)
Here it is.
(*Plucks out the morning newspaper, still folded, and begins putting everything else back in.*)

OLIVER

You've got *two* bathing suits in there?

CARRIE
(*Nodding, informatively*)
They get wet.

OLIVER
(*Also nodding, sagely*)
True.

(CARRIE *settles herself with a glass of water in each hand. Instantly the phone rings and instantly* OLIVER *darts for it, mainly to stop its ringing*)

OLIVER
Hello. Sure it's me. Who else would it be? You want me to what? Turn off your electric blanket? Ye gods, you didn't have the electric blanket on last night? Okay, if you call sixty degrees freezing. All right, all right, I'll turn it off. Oh, wait—wait—wait! That mysterious Mrs. Amagansett showed up. It's you, my dear, she wants to see. She's right out on the deck. I'll—no, hold on, I'll get her.
(*Putting down the receiver and calling out toward the deck doors*)
Oh—Madam—Miss—Miz!
(CARRIE *rises*)

CARRIE
Listen. I hate to be called Miz. It doesn't sound liberated to me. It just sounds short for manuscript.

OLIVER
Never mind that. Here, my wife is on the telephone. Why don't you talk to her?

CARRIE
Talk to her?

OLIVER
You said you wanted to talk to her.

CARRIE

Yes, but not now. I mean not here. I mean not on the telephone. Where is she?

OLIVER

She's with her mother and what difference does that make?

CARRIE

Ask to speak to her mother.

OLIVER
(*Staring at her*)
You want to speak to her mother?

CARRIE

No, *you* want to speak to her mother.

OLIVER

But I *don't* want to speak to her mother. You know, kookie is one thing. I have a feeling *you're* crazy.
(*Returns quickly to telephone*)
Nora, look—there's a small matter I want to settle here. I'll call you right back. No, I don't have to call you back. No, of course it's not anything vital. Sure I'm sure. Okay, I'll see you then.
(He *hangs up. After a very small pause, he turns to* CARRIE)
Why were you so certain that my wife wasn't with her mother?

CARRIE
(*A brief pause*)
Because she's with my husband.
(*Sudden great rush of apology as* OLIVER *looks stricken*)
Oh, I'm sorry. That was really rotten of me. That's the rottenest I've ever been. I hate rotten people. It's all this sunlight. It makes

me feel furry and light-headed and I didn't have anything to eat—
not even grapefruit—

OLIVER

Why didn't you have anything to eat?

CARRIE

Is that really your first question: why I didn't have anything to
eat?

OLIVER

I can think of another question. Does your husband work in a delicatessen?

CARRIE

No, he doesn't; why?

OLIVER

Because she's *always* stopping by the Deli.

CARRIE

Is this what you're like, is this really what you're like—cool and
creepy?

OLIVER

Look, my dear, you barged in here uninvited. May I suggest you
barge out?

CARRIE

People only call you "my dear" when they are irritated with you.

OLIVER

True.

CARRIE

But we haven't settled anything!

OLIVER

What did you have in mind? Should we buy them identical T-shirts with a scarlet "A"?

CARRIE

You know something? I don't like you.

OLIVER

Oh? Well, I'll just have to bear up.

CARRIE

The thing is, I *should* leave. I should go. I should get out of here. But I can't walk down that highway and I'm not going to sit out on that dumb deck and have you glare at me through the glass. You know, there is so much glass here! And where is that damn cab? I feel dizzy. Oh, I feel worse than dizzy. My head is rattling and grinding like a spoon that got dropped in the Disposall. Oh, my God, do you think I'm going to faint? I never fainted in my whole life—not even when I got my hand smashed in the car door. They say people fainted at *The Exorcist*. I never believed that for one minute—I never—
    (She *reels a little.* OLIVER *grabs her and helps her to the sofa*)
Oh my, oh dear, oh—
        (*This is not an act;* she *does feel faint*)

OLIVER

Look, sit back and shut up for a minute. Put your head between your legs. I'll get you something to eat.
    (*Goes into the kitchen area behind the counter so that* he *is in-and-out visible*)

CARRIE

I'm on a diet.

OLIVER

I know that. I even know which diet.

CARRIE

Oh, the water.

OLIVER

That's right.

CARRIE

I see you are going to be civilized. I'm not sure it's so civilized to be civilized *all* the time.

OLIVER
(*Handing her a plate*)

Here. Eat something and maybe you'll start making a little more sense.

CARRIE

I can't eat these eggs. They're stuffed.

OLIVER
(*Stepping into kitchen area and bringing out a cup and saucer and a pot of coffee*)

There's no mayonnaise. Just a little mustard and Worcestershire sauce. That's allowed.

CARRIE

Oh, you're on it.

OLIVER

Just for the weekend.
(*Puts coffeepot on coffee table*)

CARRIE

These are really delicious. You should have one.

OLIVER

That had been my plan.

CARRIE

I'm really a disgrace. I burst in here, interrupt your work, ruin your day, eat your lunch. I'm Carrie Sachs.

OLIVER

How do you do, Mrs. Sachs.
(*Going to phone*)
Now I'll check on your taxi.

CARRIE

Please.
(CARRIE *jumps up, shaking her skirt, looking for something.* OLIVER *frowns, puzzled by this, while he dials*)

OLIVER
(*Into phone*)
Eddie? Doctor DeVreck again—about that cab. Well, I hope so.
(*Hanging up*)
He said the cab is on its way. But they always say the cab is on the way.
(*Without a break*)
How did you find out . . . about my wife and your husband? Did he tell you?

CARRIE

(*Munching on the stuffed eggs*)

No, not exactly. What happened was, it was about eleven-thirty at night and I was there alone and the phone rang. I picked up the phone and I didn't get to say "Hello" yet because I was fishing around for this cigarette lighter I dropped. And then I heard my husband's voice. He sounded different but it was Peter, all right, and what he said was "Darling, talk to me, I just want to hear your voice." And I just . . . knew. I said, "Peter? Peter?" And he coughed and made some kind of joke. But I knew.

OLIVER

You mean he had just plain dialed the wrong number.

CARRIE

Isn't that crazy?

OLIVER

Freud would say that subconsciously he wanted you to find out.

CARRIE

Freud, hell! That's what *I* said.

OLIVER

But he admitted it.

CARRIE

Yeah. Actually, just before the phone call he was being especially sweet. He was so husbandly. You know: "Shall I get you a sweater?" "Isn't there too much sun in your eyes?" I should have noticed. It's a sign.

OLIVER
(*Hearing the echo and thinking his own thoughts as* he
removes the sunglasses)
Yes, I guess that is a sign. You should have noticed.

CARRIE
But I didn't notice anything. That's because I'm so dumb. I've always been dumb. Do you know that I am the only person in this
century that learned the facts of life from a pamphlet?

OLIVER
A pamphlet?

CARRIE
(*Nodding*)
And the worst thing of all was my grandmother gave it to me—not
even my mother—my grandmother, for God's sake! Wouldn't you
think I'd have figured out something when I read *Anna Karenina*?
But I didn't. So I sat on the cellar steps and I read this stupid
pamphlet—it was called *Marjorie May's Twelfth Birthday*—and
there were these little diagrams. You know, arrows showing which
direction the spermatozoid went. And I cried, because it was so
different from *Anna Karenina*.

OLIVER
Tolstoy would be cheered to know that.

CARRIE
But don't you see it was really idiotic? And I don't know why I
am eating these goddam eggs, I don't know why I'm on this rotten
diet, and—
(she's *weeping now*)
—the only reason he married me was because I was so fat.

OLIVER

Don't be ridiculous. Nobody ever married anybody because they were fat. And stop crying. You're going to get extra salt on everything.

CARRIE

But that really is why he married me. He was a widower and he had this little girl. I tutored her. I tutored her in math and Spanish. And I seemed so sensible and substantial. Boy, was I ever substantial! I weighed a hundred and eighty pounds. Do you believe that? If you say you believe it, I'll kill you.

OLIVER

I don't believe it. Here, have some coffee.
(*Pours some into her cup*)

CARRIE

It wasn't just that I was so fat. I was so completely different from his first wife. In the beginning I think he was relieved about that.
(She *lights a cigarette, rather shakily*)

OLIVER

Oh? What was she like?

CARRIE

Apparently she was so charming it was practically a disease. Even the hygienist who cleaned her big, white teeth fell in love with her. She could get plumbers to come on Sunday.

OLIVER

Well, that's quite a recommendation. Shall we compare her to a summer's day?

CARRIE

Except that there was one little problem. One tiny fly in this lovely ointment. It seems about every month she'd have a new lover. I mean she'd bring one back and take another one out—like library books. It got so he started to worry whenever she left the house.

OLIVER

I think I need a drink.
(*Goes toward bar*)

CARRIE

Oh, no, not on this diet!

OLIVER

You can have one ounce of liquor or one small glass of white wine. Oh, hell, I don't have any liquor!
(*Throws away two empties into a wastebasket*)

CARRIE

How come you don't have any liquor in this big, jazzy place?

OLIVER

Because my wife doesn't drink. And I didn't plan to drink this weekend. Is there anything else you'd like to know?

CARRIE

That's interesting. And she doesn't smoke, either.

OLIVER

Not any more. How do you know that?

CARRIE

Because there are no ashtrays. If she doesn't smoke and she doesn't drink, what does she do?

(*Suddenly catching the implication and jumping up*)
I'm sorry! Honestly, I didn't mean that!
   (*In her distress,* she *swings her bag so that it knocks the plate of eggs onto the floor*)
Look, I'll go. It's not just that I'm beginning to get on your nerves. I'm *on* your nerves. Good-bye and thank you for the egg. The Worcestershire sauce is a good idea.
         (She'*s practically at the door*)

OLIVER

   (*In total despair, gets a cloth to mop up the mess* she'*s made*)
You're going to go. Fine. Dandy. But where are you going to go *to?*

CARRIE

I'll just walk down the road until I find something.

OLIVER
   (*On his knees, cleaning the rug*)
It's not a road. It's the Montauk Highway. And you won't find anything. You'll just get hit by a car. And they'll take you to the nearest doctor. And, goddamit, I'm the nearest doctor. You'll be right back *here!*

CARRIE
   (*Returning, interested*)
Oh yes. I do keep forgetting you're a doctor. What kind of doctor are you?

OLIVER
   (*On the floor, crumpling, the battle lost*)
I'm a marriage counselor.

CARRIE

You're a marriage counselor?

OLIVER
(*Nodding*)

I would agree that under the circumstances it's pretty ridiculous.

CARRIE

Well, do you work? I mean does *it* work? The process. Should I come to see you?

OLIVER
(*Rising*)

No. Let me repeat. No.

CARRIE

That's a very unprofessional attitude. You don't have to *like* your patients, do you?

OLIVER

No. I don't have to like my patients. Nor do I have to treat every unbalanced person who tumbles into my lap.

CARRIE

I am neither in, nor on, nor anywhere near your lap. And I'm not unbalanced. Maybe I am.

OLIVER
(*On his way to the phone*)

What's *with* Eddie? They're always slow, but this is preposterous!
(*Dialing furiously*)

CARRIE

Why don't you let me talk to Eddie? Maybe I could get him to hurry it up.

OLIVER

(*Holding the phone in a half-lowered position to talk to
her*)
Like how?

CARRIE

I'd say I was pregnant and in a hurry to get to the hospital.

OLIVER

Are you crazy? That's every cabbie's nightmare: that some woman
will have a baby in his cab.
(*He can hear someone answering, puts receiver back to
ear*)
Eddie? Me again. No, he's *not* here. Why would I be calling if he
was here? What? What? No, she isn't. I don't care what you heard
me say, the passenger is not pregnant! Okay, but hurry.
(*Hangs up*)

CARRIE

How did you get to be a marriage counselor? How does anybody
get to be? They don't have schools for that, do they?

OLIVER

Look, I'm a psychiatrist. I treat all kinds of people.

CARRIE

If you're a psychiatrist, why don't you call yourself a psychiatrist?
It sounds more dignified.
(*She sits and fishes for a cigarette*)

OLIVER

Because lately I'm better known as a marriage counselor, and I
don't think there's anything the least bit undignified about it.

CARRIE

Better known? How did you get to be better known?

OLIVER
(*A bit sheepish*)

Well, actually—since my first book came out.

CARRIE

Oh, you wrote a book! What was the book?

OLIVER

It was called *Settled Out of Court*.

CARRIE
(*Frowning*)

Settled Out of Court.
(*It all comes back*)

Oh, I read that! I got it from the Literary Guild. Boy, if you don't mail those little cards back right away, you get the craziest books!

OLIVER

You certainly do.

CARRIE
(*Instantly apologetic*)

I didn't mean *your* book was crazy. It was sort of interesting. But that was two whole years ago. And Peter and I were still at that stage where happiness is noticeable. And I didn't know why I was reading about these mixed-up people and their mixed-up marriages. Well, now I know.

OLIVER

Yeah, now you know.
(*She jumps up suddenly, shaking her skirt again*)

Why do you jump up like that?

CARRIE

I keep losing my lighter in my skirt.

(*Retrieving it and settling again*)

The only part of your book I can remember now is the woman who complained because her husband used to show he wanted to make love by bringing a container of strawberry yogurt to bed. Why did he do that?

OLIVER

He thought it gave him immediate energy.

CARRIE

Is that true? Is that scientific?

OLIVER

That's hardly the point. The point is, it's not very romantic.

CARRIE

Do you make these things up?

OLIVER

No.

CARRIE

But you must make the people up.

OLIVER

What do you mean?

CARRIE

Well, you use names, and you can't use the people's real names or they'd sue. I'd hate to be one of your patients. I'd worry that I wasn't going to be a good story. Oh dear, maybe I'll be in one of your books, slightly disguised: "Sally, bursting in like a raving maniac, definitely flabby from her recent weight loss, her body a question mark expressing fear, doubt, pain. . . ."

OLIVER
(*Finally exploding*)

Look! Go get yourself killed on the Montauk Highway. What's it to me? Now I absolutely have to have a drink, and if you would shut up for one minute I would be endlessly in your debt.
(*Has gone to phone, dials*)

CARRIE

You're going to order some? That'll take—

OLIVER
(*To her*)

Just one minute. Please. Go to the bathroom. Go read a book.
(*Turns to phone again*)

Leo? It's Oliver upstairs. I just wanted to be sure somebody was there. Can I come down and borrow some bourbon? Don't be silly, I can come down. It doesn't matter. Any kind—Old Taylor, Old Grand-Dad, Old Anybody. Okay, but don't bring me one of those hulking half-gallon jugs. I just want a little bit. Hell, a little bit is a little bit!

> (*While* OLIVER *is talking on the phone,* CARRIE *stands up to reach for coffeepot, starts to pour herself more coffee. But she tips the pot too far forward, so that the percolator comes apart, the section containing the coffee grounds splattering all over the floor. Frantically, she tries to clean up while* OLIVER *is still talking on the phone, but burns her fingers in the process. Finally she just kicks the remains of the pot under the coffee table and, as* OLIVER *hangs up, faces him with great innocence, as though nothing had happened.* OLIVER *does see the mess, and closes his eyes in despair*)

CARRIE
(*Innocently*)

Who was that?

OLIVER

That was my landlord. He lives downstairs.

CARRIE

I didn't notice there was an apartment down there.

OLIVER

It's a room—one big room. With some wicker furniture and all the liquor in America.

CARRIE

Is he a lush?

OLIVER
(*Wearily*)

No, it's cheaper by the jug.

CARRIE
(*Distracting him*)

Do you know what is sad about your book?

OLIVER

Everything, I gather.

CARRIE

I mean sad-wistful. Most of the people who come to you are women. I guess that means that women are more helpless, more desperate.

OLIVER

No, they're just more practical. If the dishwasher breaks, a woman calls a plumber. A man says, "I'll look into it." Five days later he looks into it with a putty knife—and now it needs a whole new unit. Women are quicker to get professional help.

CARRIE

These women that come to you—do they have sexual problems?

OLIVER

Sometimes.

CARRIE

Do you—uh—console them?

OLIVER

What you really mean is do I sleep with them.

CARRIE

I didn't mean that.

OLIVER

Yes, you did. And no, I don't. I don't think bartenders should drink.

CARRIE

I don't get it.

(*Very slight pause*)

I get it. You think it's unsuitable.

OLIVER

And unethical. And, as a matter of fact, illegal.

CARRIE

Can I ask you one last question?

OLIVER

No.

CARRIE

But this is really important. It's my whole life that's breaking down. Peter won't talk to me. We never talk about important things. The thing is, I talk, and he sort of smiles and takes his glasses off and listens to me. I don't understand why he takes his glasses off to listen. And then he chews on the earpiece, and he can actually talk this way.

(She *demonstrates with a pair of sunglasses from her pocket*)

Why does he do that? I bet there's some deep psychological reason.

OLIVER

Or did he just recently stop smoking?

CARRIE

As a matter of fact, he did! That's really very perceptive of you. I should take you more seriously.

OLIVER

(*Leaning forward and staring at her*)

I don't want your cab to come. I think you should stay on for the whole summer. I think we should grow old together.

CARRIE

(*Hearing the sarcasm*)

Oh, dear—

OLIVER

But I'm serious. This is a valuable experience. I've never had a nervous breakdown before. I've always felt out of things.

CARRIE
(*Trying to change the subject*)
Listen, your wife called before. What did she call about?

OLIVER
(*Surprised and fussed*)
That's right, she called. What *did* she call about? Oh, the electric blanket! She wanted me to turn it off.
(*Has started toward the bedroom*)

CARRIE
How do you stand an electric blanket in this weather?

OLIVER
(*Halting in the archway, explaining as to a child*)
I don't have to stand it. It's in her room.

CARRIE
(*Instantly picking up the implications*)
In *her* room? I guess *you* don't talk about the important things either.

OLIVER
(*Advancing on her*)
Now, look—

CARRIE
(*Standing her ground*)
You look! You're in an impossible situation. Your wife plays around, she sleeps in a different room, and you're a marriage counselor. I think I could help you.

OLIVER
You—*you* could help *me!*

CARRIE

Well, you couldn't go see another marriage counselor, could you? You're a nervous wreck! Look at the way you're twisting that paper clip!

(OLIVER *notices* he *is doing just that, throws it on desk*)

You've probably got hundreds of mangled paper clips all over this house! How old are you? Forty-three, forty-four—?

OLIVER

I'm thirty-six.

CARRIE

That's stress. It makes you look older.

OLIVER

I assure you, Mrs. Sachs, I was a perfect 36 before you swooped in on me—

CARRIE

Look, call me Carrie. It makes more sense now that we're going to get to know each other.

OLIVER

We are not. We are absolutely by God not!

CARRIE

But you need help.

OLIVER
(*Eyes wide, a little madly*)

Oh, I do, I do! I sure as hell do!
(*Has gone to the open window and is shouting down-ward*)

Leo! Lee—OHHH!! Where the hell are you?

(*Meanwhile* LEO SIMPSON *has appeared on the deck behind him.* He *comes in, carrying a Pyrex measuring cup.* CARRIE *is not in his line of vision*)

LEO

Why are you *bellowing?* We'll have the harbor police in here. I knew you wanted a drink. I didn't think you were going into withdrawal.

OLIVER
(*Snatching the cup and taking it to the bar*)

Leo, don't chatter. I'm a good tenant. You know I'm a good tenant. I water your damn plants. I feed them Miracle-Gro. When it rains, I get up in the middle of the night and close the windows. I never leave pillows out on the deck—

LEO

You're hysterical.

OLIVER
(*Forgetting the drink in his urgency*)

I am. That's why you have to do something for me.
(*Pointing to* CARRIE)

You must drive this woman to the station—or wherever—and I will make it up to you in little ways. I'll put in new shelf paper, I'll clean the oven—

CARRIE
(*Coming forward, now that* she's *had a look*)

Leo, good heavens! Leo Simpson!

LEO
(*Spinning toward her*)

Carrie, honey—it's you! Or is it? It can't be. Where's the rest of you? Darling, the half that's left is terrific.

CARRIE
(*Runs to embrace him*)

Leo—dear, dear Leo, I haven't seen you since we took the course at the New School.

LEO
(*Nodding*)

I was touring.
(*Puts his arms around her.* OLIVER *watches in surprise*)
Here, let me try out this new waistline. A size 8! What hath God wrought? It's a miracle. You went to Lourdes.

CARRIE

Oh, I drank all this water and ate six million eggs.

LEO

It was worth it!

CARRIE

But you own this house? How can an actor afford this big, jazzy place?

LEO

I can't. That's why I rent it in the summer.

OLIVER

For a lot of money.

LEO
(*To* OLIVER)

This is your third summer. If you could find a cheaper place that was just as gorgeous, you'd have taken it.
(*To* CARRIE)
Can I offer you some of his bourbon—my bourbon—our bourbon?

CARRIE

No, thank you.

OLIVER
(*Elaborate sarcasm, slightly hysterical*)
Have a drink! Both of you! Sit down. Put your feet up! Be comfortable!
(*Going toward desk, and riffling papers*)
It doesn't matter if I never finish these galleys! What matters is that you young people have a happy reunion!

LEO
(*To* CARRIE, *puzzled by the blowoff*)
Hey, what are you doing here with Oliver?

OLIVER
(*Has dropped into chair at desk, but looks up instantly, alerted, warning* CARRIE)
We're not going to discuss that, are we?

CARRIE
Are you looking at me? Oh, no, never!
(*Back to* LEO, *nervously, changing the subject*)
Oh, listen, I saw the *Romeo and Juliet* in the Park. You were very good as Benvolio.
(*They do sit on sofa as they chat*)

LEO
Don't lie. In four hundred years nobody's been good as Benvolio.

CARRIE
Well, you were definitely the loudest one.

LEO
That helps?

CARRIE

In Central Park, with all those airplanes zooming over, it certainly does.

(OLIVER *is trying to work*)

LEO

I only agreed to play it because they let me understudy Paul Severn. He was the Romeo. And I figured I'd get to play the part because Paul has this reputation of being sick a lot.

CARRIE

Did he get sick?

LEO

Yes, he got ptomaine poisoning. He ate half of a shrimp salad sandwich that was spoiled.

CARRIE

Well, how *were* you?

LEO

I ate the other half.

CARRIE

Leo, that is the story of your life. If you ever write a book, that's what you can call it: *I Ate the Other Half.*

OLIVER

(*Pushing his chair back from desk in desperation, to* LEO)

Would you drive your friend, Mrs. Sachs, to wherever she wants to go?

LEO

Oh, gee—my car's in the shop—
       (*Finally catches the name*)
Mrs. Sachs? Carrie, you're married! I didn't know.

CARRIE

My picture was in the *Times*—"Miss Waters to Wed."

LEO

Well, who is he, what does he do?

CARRIE

His name is Peter Sachs. He doesn't exactly do anything. He's rich
for a living.

LEO

Terrific. Good for him.

CARRIE

He'd hate me to say that. He's sort of an art dealer.

LEO

How come I didn't get invited to the wedding?

CARRIE

You did. I called you. I got that model you were living with—
Melinda? She told me you were at the Pittsburgh Playhouse.
How's Melinda?

LEO

Who knows? She went to the Cannes film festival last year and
never came back.
       (LEO *picks up a box of fish food next to the fish tank*)

OLIVER

They're *fed!*

LEO
(*To* CARRIE, *putting the fish food down*)
I got left with her mynah bird and a closetful of very expensive dresses. I think I'll have a garage sale.
(LEO *is now poking his finger into the soil around the plant on the mantel*)

OLIVER

They're watered!

LEO

Yes. Nice and moist.

CARRIE
(*To* OLIVER)
Listen, you should go to the bedroom and turn off that electric blanket.

OLIVER
(*Jumping up*)
Oh, Lord, yes!
(OLIVER *hurries off to the bedroom.* CARRIE *grabs* LEO's *arm*)

CARRIE
(*Rather furtively and urgently*)
Leo—

LEO
(*Puzzled, adopting her secretive tone*)
What's with the electric blanket?

CARRIE

I just wanted to get rid of him.

LEO

You wanted to what?

CARRIE

Please. Don't talk. Don't ask questions. We've only got a minute. Oh, Leo, Dr. DeVreck and I—we're in a mess!

LEO
(*Relaxing*)
You and Oliver? I don't believe it. You—have become a swinger?

CARRIE
(*Hurrying on*)
You're talking. Don't talk. Just tell me about his wife.

LEO

In sign language?

CARRIE
(*After a quick, apprehensive glance toward the front door*)
Leo, please, I'm desperate! Just tell me about his wife.

LEO

What do you want to know?

CARRIE

What is she like?

LEO

She's terrific. I'm crazy about her.

CARRIE
(*With a sigh*)

You, too. And I bet she can get plumbers on Sunday. Poor me.
Poor Oliver.

LEO

What's going on here? Are you both double agents?

CARRIE

You heard him. I'm sworn to silence.

LEO
(*As though scandalized*)

And this is a man I trusted! My very own shrink, who helped me.

CARRIE

You were his patient?

LEO

I lost Melinda. I had to have somebody. In his office he seems so
righteous, sitting there underneath that painting of Saint Sebastian.
(*Shaking his head*)

All those arrows.
(*Reverting to* CARRIE)

Now, level with me—

(*The telephone rings as* OLIVER *returns from the bedroom*)

OLIVER

Leo, answer it and say I'm out.

LEO

You answer it and say you're out.

CARRIE

I'll answer it.

OLIVER
(*Frantic*)

She can't answer it! She'll turn back into Mrs. Amagansett—Leo, *please!*

LEO
(*Picking up phone and assuming a voice*)

The number you have reached is not a working number.
(*Back to his own voice*)

Yeah, it's Leo. I'm up here bringing Oliver some bourbon. I presume he wanted to drink it. Yeah. Okay, I'll ask him.
(*To* OLIVER)

It's Nora. She's on her way home. She's at the Deli. She wants to know if you want anything.

OLIVER

Nothing. Just peace and quiet.

LEO
(*Into the phone*)

Just English muffins. Okay.
(*Hangs up*)

OLIVER

I don't want English muffins.

LEO

I do.

CARRIE
(*Disturbed*)

She's coming. She'll *be* here.

LEO
(*Noticing* CARRIE's *distress*)
Come on, Carrie, I'll take you out of all this. I'll show you my rare coin collection—

CARRIE
(*As* LEO *pulls her toward deck*)
Leo, you don't still save all those pennies in bottles—!

OLIVER
(*Not looking up from the galleys* he's *returned to*)
You haven't heard. He's had the bottles wired. Now they're lamps.

LEO
And I'll whip us up a steak tartare!

CARRIE
(*Holding back, for reasons of her own*)
Oh no, I don't think I can—

LEO
Of course you can. It's the very thing for your diet. Sirloin, raw egg, onion—!
(*Suddenly*)
Oh, wait! I can't take her down there!

OLIVER
(*Head up, firmly*)
Yes, you can.

LEO
The place is a mess today.

OLIVER
Today? Every day.

LEO

I've been sorting my laundry. Everything dirty since Memorial Day is in little piles all over the floor. Look, just give me three minutes. I'll shovel up all that stuff and throw it in the bathroom. Carrie, if you want to go to the bathroom, use his bathroom.

OLIVER
(*Past patience, rising*)
Look, I can take my proofs and *I* can go down there.

LEO
(*Quickly*)
Going, going, gone—

> (*And* LEO *is gone, down the deck stairs.* OLIVER *at once stalks to where* CARRIE *is standing. He elaborately unstraps his wristwatch and places it where* she *can keep an eye on it*)

OLIVER
Leo said three minutes.
> (*Turns to go to desk.* CARRIE *sits, instantly, erect in a high-backed chair*)

CARRIE
Doctor DeVreck, I'm going to say something that will surprise you.

OLIVER
Surprise me? I don't think so. As far as you're concerned, I've kind of leveled off.

CARRIE
I'm not going downstairs with Leo. I'm going to stay right here and meet your wife.

OLIVER

The hell you are! No, ma'am, no way!

CARRIE

A minute ago you were saying that women were so practical. I thought you admired that quality. Now here I am being absolutely practical and you seem fussed.

OLIVER

Fussed? I'm not fussed!

CARRIE

Well, you're grinding your teeth. You shouldn't do that. You could alter your bite. That happened to a friend of mine. He had to go to a dentist for months. And he had to keep this crazy plastic thing in his mouth while he slept. It was terrible. Well?

OLIVER

I think I've forgotten the subject of this conversation.

CARRIE

No you haven't. Your wife will be here in a few minutes. And I have to see her; *I will* see her!

OLIVER

Mrs. Sachs, it is clear to me that down through all eternity I can't, of course, keep you from talking to my wife. But you can do it on your time and her time. Not my time.

CARRIE

You don't have to be here. You can go down and talk to Leo.

OLIVER

I *could* give you the name of a good therapist, but I doubt that would help.

*(Putting his hand on her elbow and leading her toward
the deck)*

You just run right along. Remember, you have the number here.
You call her and give her your correct name and make an appointment.

CARRIE
*(Really mad for the first time, pulling away and throw-
ing her bag on the floor)*

Don't put your hand on me! You're impossible. You have the
blood temperature of a fish. "Make an appointment," for heaven's
sake! You'd think I was looking for a job. We're talking about
your wife. You should be heartbroken. Instead, you're just faintly
irritated—like you'd just pushed the down button and the elevator
went up.

OLIVER
(Curtly)

You through?

CARRIE

No, I haven't even started. Mrs. DeVreck wouldn't make an appointment with me!

OLIVER

What makes you so sure of that?

CARRIE

Because if she has any decency at all, she'd feel too guilty to see
me! And I have to believe that she is somehow or other a decent
person, because otherwise somebody as nice as Peter is . . .
wouldn't like her.

*(Starts to cry, drops to her knees beside her bag, sitting
on her heels)*

"Like her," I say. "Like her"! Poor Peter, poor thin-for-nothing me—he loves her. He told me he loves her. He shouldn't have told me that. He should *never* have told me.

OLIVER
(*Quietly, seriously*)
Look, I am really sorry. Really. And I ask you to believe that I am not exactly the cold haddock I appear to be. After a while, you find ways to protect yourself. Let's just say that my heart has cried wolf too often.

CARRIE
But you do want her back?

OLIVER
She hasn't gone anywhere.

CARRIE
That's a silly statement! Do they have to fly to Bermuda to make it real for you? You just want this thing to blow over. I want it to *be* over. Don't you?

OLIVER
Yes, yes, all right, yes. But what could you say to her that I couldn't say?

CARRIE
I could explain to her the difference between her situation and my situation. Peter wouldn't tell her. He'd be too loyal. And isn't that crazy? I still think of Peter as loyal.

OLIVER
And what is this difference?

CARRIE

You've just met me. But can't you tell! My problem first, last and always is that I am a beautiful person. Everybody says so.
(*Imitating*)
"Carrie is a beautiful person."

OLIVER

And what does that mean?

CARRIE

First it means that I'm not beautiful. And the rest of it means that I'm quick and reliable and I have a good disposition. Exactly the qualities you'd look for if you were buying a Labrador retriever.

OLIVER

Oh, come on, now—!
(*Without thinking, he pats her gently on the head, almost as though she were a household pet. She doesn't notice, plunges on*)

CARRIE

But it's true!

OLIVER

I hope you hear yourself. You sound like poor, pitiful Pearl.

CARRIE

I'm just trying to sound realistic. Peter is the only man that's ever been in my life. If he hadn't come along, I would have gone on being what I always was: an air fern.

OLIVER

A what?

CARRIE

An air fern.

OLIVER

What's an air fern?

CARRIE

It's a fern—you know, a plant. But it doesn't have any roots. And
you don't have to water it. It lives on air. Somebody gave me one
once and I put it in this Lenox teacup. But I never liked it. It was
this awful fake green. I really thought it was artificial. And then
one day I noticed it had turned brown. That was because it was
dead. That's the only way I knew it *had* been alive. You know
there are *people* like that?

OLIVER

Actually, there is something not entirely unappealing about you,
Carrie. I think your grief is real. I wish I could help you.

CARRIE

Then leave me alone with your wife.

OLIVER

What could you *hope* to accomplish?

CARRIE

I could make it clear that she *can* replace Peter. But *I* can't. So
she's got to let him go.
     (Mind clicking over again)
Oh, I just had another idea.

OLIVER
    (Alarmed)
Don't tell me. Please don't tell me!

CARRIE

I'm just wondering. Now that I'm thin—maybe Leo would have an affair with me. That would make Peter think twice.

OLIVER

I wouldn't advise it.

CARRIE

Why not—if I can swing it?

OLIVER

Because this fighting fire with fire is a very tricky business. If things don't exactly mesh, you just double the problem.

CARRIE

You're talking about two wrongs not making a right.

OLIVER

Not at all. I'm talking about two fires. When I was in Boy Scout camp, about a million years ago, we had a fire break out in the dry grass behind the cabins. It was really kind of scary. And our counselor, who was something of a jerk anyway, got the idea of digging a trench and starting another fire a hundred yards away. Except that he didn't start the second fire in the right place. The next thing, we had two fires that passed each other. Thank God we got the fire department.

CARRIE

But what have fires got to do with people?

OLIVER

Not a hell of a lot. I was just trying to make an analogy.

CARRIE

Don't get mad. I'm really trying to understand this.

OLIVER

All I'm saying is that your little scheme could backfire. Your husband might feel relieved—and justified.

CARRIE
(She *is unmistakably working it out*)
But if the fire was set in the right place, if things really meshed—

OLIVER

Even if they meshed, you're still playing with fire.

CARRIE
(She*'s got it*)
The thing is—you've got to get it closer. Like if you and I had an affair, that would be closer.

OLIVER

Yes.
(*Then notices her expression*)
You're actually considering that! No—the answer is no! I'm all tied up for the next couple of years.

CARRIE

The irony of it doesn't appeal to you? I know *I* don't appeal to you.

OLIVER

Listen, whenever you meet my wife—it's clear you are going to do so with or without my blessing—revert to your original plan. You were going to appeal to her sense of fair play. Actually, Nora does have a sense of fair play.
(*A little bitterly*)
More or less. Anyway, you are going to remind her of her many options—and your more limited ones. And ask her to let your husband off the leash.

(*Phone rings*)

Damn!

(He *goes to it*)

CARRIE
(*Debating with herself*)

I don't know. . . .

OLIVER
(*Into phone*)

Hello. Mrs. Adams? Yes, yes, of course I remember. Now, wait, wait, wait. You've got to stop crying or I can't hear you. No, no, I don't think you're dying. What did you take? Well, look at the bottle, it says on the bottle. Why did you throw it away? Like a little yellow aspirin? That's Valium. How many did you take? Three. That's only fifteen milligrams. You're not dying, you're just relaxing. Look, Mrs. Adams—stay right there. I'll pick up this phone in another room. Okay—don't go—I'll be with you—

(*To* CARRIE *as he heads for bedroom*)

I've got to—

CARRIE

I know. I'll hang this up as soon as you pick up the other one.

(*As* OLIVER *disappears into bedroom area,* CARRIE *runs to the phone, listens for a second until* OLIVER *has obviously picked up his end, then hangs up. At the same time, there is an urgent sound of a foot kicking at the front door. As* CARRIE *starts toward it, we hear:*)

NORA (Off)

Hey, Oliver! Get the door, will you? I've got both hands full!

(CARRIE *hesitates at the door for a split second, realizing that this may be* NORA, *then hospitably opens it.*

NORA *does appear, with both arms overloaded with wobbly shopping bags*)

CARRIE

Oh, hello, Mrs. DeVreck. Come right in. Here, let me take one of those.

NORA

(*As* CARRIE *quickly snatches one of the bags from her*)
Well, you are the soul of hospitality! And who are you? And where is my husband?

CARRIE

He's in the bedroom.
(*Turns her attention to unloading one bag*)

NORA

(*There's something* she *doesn't like about this*)
In the bedroom?
(*Heading for it*)
Oliver! Oliver!

CARRIE

(*Grabbing her arm*)
Wait, wait—please. He's on the phone. But he knows I'm going to talk to you. We agreed to that.

NORA

And does any part of this agreement include telling me who you are? Oh, of course. How slow-witted I am! You are Mrs. Amagansett.

CARRIE

But you didn't believe that for a minute. I could tell by the way you underlined the word "who." You said . . .

> (*Imitating her on phone*)

"Who?"

> (*Extending her hand suddenly*)

I'm Carrie Sachs. How do you do?

NORA

> (*Startled, ignoring the hand*)

You're Peter's wife?

CARRIE

And you're Peter's girl friend. This bag feels cold. I'm going to put it in the kitchen for you.

> (*Taking it from the counter toward where refrigerator might be, off*)

This stuff could melt. They say you can refreeze things, but I wouldn't.

> (*She keeps popping back and forth*)

Let me get that other bag. I notice you have skim milk in here. I notice things like that because of all my diets.

NORA

Mrs. Sachs, won't you sit down? And let me explain about that foolish phone call Peter made.

> (*She sits, trying to seem composed*)

CARRIE

> (*Keeping at work on the grocery bags to overcome her nervousness, all of which is making* NORA *nervous*)

No, thank you, I've been sitting all day—

NORA

I don't know exactly what to say—

> (*And it's difficult for her to think with* CARRIE *so busy*)

Please put the groceries down. Please sit down.

CARRIE

(*Deposits grocery bag on small table, turns toward* NORA)

I'd rather stand.

NORA

(*Rising, and speaking more firmly*)

Please sit down.

CARRIE

(*About to take off again*)

I think I'd better—

NORA

(*Swiftly intercepting her, speaking to her as though training a dog*)

Sit!

(CARRIE *does sit, reluctantly, stiffly*)

Look, you must believe me. The whole thing between Peter and me was nothing. One day my car broke down in front of the fish market, so I walked over to the cab stand. Naturally, there were no cabs—

(*She, too, has seated herself, on the sofa, trying to be easy*)

CARRIE

They're *never!* It's really a disgrace, the cab situation.

NORA

(*Going on, with an effort*)

So a car pulled up and this man said, "I'm not a taxi, I'm Peter Sachs, but if you're going anywhere down the Montauk I'd be happy to drop you." So I got in the car.

CARRIE

That messy car! Peter's so ambivalent about being rich. Because it's a Mercedes, he won't ever get it washed. And then that front seat—all littered with sneakers and old road maps! I'd rather have a clean Chevy.

(She *takes out a cigarette. Without a word,* NORA—*whose nerves have just snapped—shifts closer to* CARRIE, *snatches* CARRIE's *pack of cigarettes and, her hand noticeably trembling, lights up.* She *takes a deep drag and is finally able to continue*)

NORA

In any case, he said he was suddenly starving, and so was I, and so we had lunch. We've had lunch several times since—
    (*Suddenly she breaks off, gets to her feet, changes her tone entirely*)
Look. This is too important to lie about. One day we were walking back to the car. And I guess he wanted to know what time it was. Anyway, he reached down and picked up my wrist to look at my watch—he wasn't wearing one. It was as simple as that. He was holding my wrist and we didn't say anything. But I knew what was going to happen and I was so happy . . . and so sorry.

CARRIE

(*Affected, covering it by jumping up and snatching a magazine out of a floor rack*)
That bag is beginning to make a puddle.

NORA

What are you doing?

CARRIE

(*Slipping magazine under the bag on table*)
I'm just putting a magazine under here. You'll get a white ring. Of

course, you can get it out with lemon oil. But sometimes it takes two applications.

(*Sits down again abruptly, facing* NORA *as though nothing had been interrupted*)

NORA
(*Deep breath, making a last-ditch effort*)
Look, what I'm trying to tell you is—I think I'm in love with Peter.
(*Forcing herself*)
I *am* in love with Peter.

(CARRIE *is on her feet again*)

Now what are you doing?

CARRIE
(*It takes a little more effort for her to invent just now, but* she *plunges on*)
I just wanted to see if it was this week's issue of *Time* I put under there. It'll get damp.
(*She retrieves the magazine from under the bag and looks at its cover*)
Bruce Springsteen?
(*Looks at the date*)
Oh no, this is November 1978.
(*Putting the magazine back under the bag, and gathering steam again*)
You know, I have this friend who keeps really old copies of *Time* and *Newsweek*. I mean like twenty years old. He keeps them in the bathroom, and then when he can't sleep he gets up and reads all about the Berlin airlift or the Suez crisis. He says it's very relaxing at four-thirty in the morning—because, you see, it's all over now.

NORA
(*Really baffled*)

I don't get this. You seem more concerned about my defrosting vegetables than you do about your husband.

CARRIE

Oh, dear, is that the way it seems? Not at all. Of course, I do worry about things that drip. But the truth is that right now I'm sort of using it as a delaying tactic because I'm so embarrassed.

NORA

I don't understand. Why are *you* embarrassed?

CARRIE

Because I know all that. Peter told me. Well, not about the wrist-watch, but everything else. But that's just half the story. And I can feel it in my bones you don't have a clue about the other half.

NORA

What other half? What are you talking about?

CARRIE

That's what I figured. You don't know. And I don't want to be the one that has to tell you. Though, in all the circumstances, there's no reason why *we* should feel guilty.

NORA

Can I try to pin this down? *Who* is we?

CARRIE

Me and Oliver.

NORA

You and Oliver what?

CARRIE

The simple answer to that is yes. We are.

NORA

(*Getting the general idea, and totally incredulous*)
You and Oliver?

CARRIE

You're thinking the worst. You're right.

NORA

(*Getting to her feet*)
Is that so? Well, I think I will take these into the kitchen.
(*Moves remaining bag of groceries from table*)

CARRIE

You don't ask any questions. Like how did we meet and when did it all happen.

NORA

I have every confidence you are about to tell me.
(*Returns with a towel, wipes table*)

CARRIE

You're so calm. And I bet you never ate a Ry-Krisp in your life.

NORA

What has that got to do with anything?

CARRIE

A lot. Everything.

NORA

All right. Where did you meet?

CARRIE

In his office. I was a patient.

(*Sits on the sofa*)

NORA

(*Skeptically*)

Really? Now, why did I get the definite impression when I phoned Oliver that he had never laid eyes on you before?

CARRIE

(*As though ashamed for* OLIVER)

Yes, I heard what he said. It's terrible the way love makes you deceitful. I was a patient, all right. I'll never forget how I suffered in that office, sitting under that weird painting of Saint Sebastian.

(*She's done a good enough job of remembering* LEO's *description*)

NORA

(*Forced to buy it, so far*)

All right, you *were* a patient—

CARRIE

Of course, it started out on a completely impersonal, professional basis—

NORA

You mean he did not hurl you to the carpet during your first appointment.

CARRIE

(*Crossing her legs elaborately and adopting a very worldly posture*)

I suppose I deserve the sarcasm. But don't you want to know how it developed?

NORA

You mean this thing has a plot?

CARRIE

A plot? You know, that's sort of funny.

NORA

I didn't think so, but then I frequently miss things.

CARRIE

Of course it's not funny. It's a disgrace.
(She *has a new thought*)
Oh, I just thought of something terrible!

NORA

Something *else* terrible?

CARRIE

Do you think that's why Peter doesn't wear a wristwatch? So he
can pick up girls?

NORA
(*Irked*)

I'm hardly a girl, and I don't really think I qualify as a pickup!
Peter doesn't wear a watch because he is a very relaxed person.
He doesn't want to know every five minutes what time is it, what
time is it? Oliver, on the other hand, is the kind of man who always wears his watch—

CARRIE
(*Stealing a sudden glance at* OLIVER's *watch, which is
still on the arm of the chair where* he *put it, within
reach*)
Always?

NORA

Except when he goes to bed. Otherwise, he never takes it off. He—

(CARRIE *has furtively, but not really furtively, palmed* OLIVER's *wristwatch.*

And NORA *has broken off her speech because she's noticed the sudden movement. She stares at* CARRIE, *quizzically. Then she crosses to her, stands directly in front of her, and holds out her hand.*

Caught, CARRIE *gives up* OLIVER's *wristwatch, a little-girl-guilty expression written all over her face.* NORA *stares at the watch)*

CARRIE

I'm speechless.

NORA

I'd like to think so. You really are quite a little package, aren't you?

CARRIE

Actually, we have a lot in common. You're the other woman. And *I'm* the other woman. For me, that's progress.

(OLIVER *finally returns from his call in the bedroom)*

OLIVER

Thank God that's over. Oh, Nora, you're back!

CARRIE

Is she all right? The woman on the telephone?

NORA

Oliver, you do have a way of bursting in just as the conversation is getting interesting—

OLIVER
(*Frowning as* he *realizes that something has gone on,
turns to* CARRIE)
I thought it was absolutely clear that you would talk to my wife at
some other time—in some other place.

NORA
Is it your feeling that a different setting would improve her story?

CARRIE
Listen, I had to let her in! She had all these groceries and it's her
house!

NORA
My house and—oh, dear, this sounds quaint—my husband.

OLIVER
Something's gone off the track here. You've lost me.

NORA
(*Pointedly*)
So I gather.

OLIVER
All right, would one of you care to read me the minutes of the last
meeting?

CARRIE
Well, actually—

NORA
(*Interrupting briskly*)
Let me. Mrs. Sachs seems to have trouble with her sentences. She
tends to lose interest after she gets to the verb.

CARRIE

That's probably true.

NORA
(*Continuing, with attention to* CARRIE)
In any case, she would like me to believe that after a period of being your patient, she has graduated to being your mistress.

OLIVER
(*Shocked*)

Carrie!

CARRIE
(*Anxiously trying to clue* OLIVER *in*)
Remember two fires!

OLIVER
(*To* NORA, *exploding*)
But you didn't believe her—you don't believe her—!

NORA

Of course not.

CARRIE

You would have believed me on the telephone. In real life, I don't make a very good impression. I look like a story in the *News* about unwed mothers.

NORA

Mrs. Sachs, I am not clairvoyant and in ten minutes I don't pretend to have any clear impression of you—

CARRIE

More time wouldn't help.

NORA
(*Ignoring the last remark*)

But I do, of course, know my husband. And I know him to be incapable of what you are suggesting. It's simply not in him.

CARRIE

Why? He's too ethical?

NORA

With a patient, of course. And with anybody else, he's too—too—
(*She's groping for the word*)

OLIVER
(*A bit sharply, interested now*)

Too what?

NORA

Too repressed. Too rigid. *And,* I would think, too uninterested.

CARRIE

Oliver! I'm surprised.
(*And she is, too*)

OLIVER
(*Still staring at* NORA *but holding a hand up to silence* CARRIE)

Now, wait just a minute. . . .
(*To* NORA, *puzzled but challenging*)

Whatever made you say that? You've known all along that I've had affairs from time to time.

NORA

No, I did not know—

OLIVER

Come on, now. Hardly a week passes that we don't have a little two-minute editorial about my many meaningful relationships. Why, just this morning you—

NORA

I know what I said—what I say. But I never believed it!

OLIVER
(*Flaring again*)

Then, why, why did you say it?

NORA

Because you expected me to.

OLIVER
(*Dumfounded*)

I expected you to!

CARRIE
(*Now eager to get out of this situation, grabbing her bag*)

Look, I'm going to go. Leo's got this steak tartare waiting for me. It'll get cold. I mean it'll get warm. Okay? 'Bye!
(CARRIE *starts rapidly toward the deck doors.* OLIVER *turns toward her and calls, firmly*)

OLIVER

Carrie!

(She *halts at the doors;* he *goes to her*)

It's going to be all right—don't be flustered. I told you it would be very hard for my wife to accept. But your instinct to tell her the truth was obviously the right one.

CARRIE
(*Gasping a little*)
You think?

OLIVER
I do. I was trying to be protective. I was merely being dishonest. This arrangement we have here was in trouble long before you came into the picture. So, when will I see you again?

CARRIE
(*Things are getting past her*)
Uh—later—I guess—

OLIVER
(*His hands clasping her shoulders*)
You *guess!* But it's out in the open! There's no need to hide it any more. There's no need to be furtive—is there?
(*Giving her a shake, happily*)
Is there?

CARRIE
(*Shakes her head, finally manages to get out a small:*)
N-no.

OLIVER
(*Cupping her chin in his hand*)
So. As soon as you're through with Leo and your steak, come up —or call me.
(OLIVER *kisses her lightly but definitely on the lips*)
Okay?
(*Escorting her onto deck*)

CARRIE
(*Fearfully, rather hushed*)
You're certain it's all right?

OLIVER

Absolutely. See you later, baby.

(CARRIE *goes down the deck stairs.* OLIVER *watches after her a moment; then, with a great show of casualness, turns in toward* NORA)

NORA

"See you later, baby"? That may be harder to believe than anything.
(*Pacing. In effect,* they're beginning to circle one another warily)
Do I take it that you are actually sleeping with that . . . waif?

OLIVER

What really shocks you—her waifness or my waywardness?

NORA

(*Slipping from sarcasm to anger*)
Oh, we *are* balancing our phrases, aren't we? Well, stop it. You're not giving an interview. Just tell me what's going on!

OLIVER

Tell you! But you know!

NORA

I don't *know* anything. I heard what she said and what you said. It all sounds extremely farfetched.

OLIVER

For one so repressed as I? And whatever made you say *that?*
(OLIVER *becomes increasingly angry as it all comes back to him*)
For that matter, what in God's name did you mean when you said

I expected you—presumably *wanted* you—to carry on about my nonexistent love affairs? What the hell sense could that make?

NORA

You've heard of role playing? Surely I picked up the term from you. Well, my role has always been to assure you daily that you are hounded by females who long only to be yours. And that I am sick with jealousy about the whole situation. And that I am—

OLIVER
(*Cutting her off*)

Wait, just wait. You're giving me an awful lot to digest in one swallow. You're saying that I think I am hounded by available, accessible women. No, you're saying I *want* to think—

NORA

That's right. You've got it.

OLIVER

And why do I want to think that? Obviously you've given this much thought. Perhaps you'd like to explain.

NORA

I shouldn't have to explain anything. You're the one who was five years in analysis. And you want *me* to tell you why you didn't turn out to be a sex symbol!

OLIVER

Sex symbol? You've been reading the *National Enquirer* again.

NORA

You know what I mean.

OLIVER

Sure. You mean I'm not sexually desirable.

NORA

It would help a little if you'd *listen*. I think you're sexually desirable. *You* don't. And if you ask me *why* again, I'll scream—

OLIVER

Well, prepare to scream, because I'm going to ask you.

NORA

How do I know? Maybe it all goes back to when you wanted to be a big, blond jock and you were a skinny bookworm with such a bad overbite that all the kids called you Bunny.

OLIVER

Now, that's a giant stride down Memory Lane! I forgot that I ever told you that.

NORA

Well, obviously you did.

OLIVER

And that was a mistake, since it's totally irrelevant. My overbite was completely corrected by an excellent orthodontist by the time I was fifteen.
      (*Making a grimace that shows his teeth*)
My bite is perfect. Perhaps it's my bark.

NORA

Oh, shut up.

OLIVER

You see what we have here—a classic case of mistaken identity. Here you were, loyally trying to build up my confidence and all along I thought your recriminations were part of a smoke screen to cover up your own little affair with Peter Sachs!

NORA
(*Grasping* he*'s known more than* she *thought*)
You knew about him?

OLIVER
I didn't know his name, but I have learned that by the time my snoring gets so bad that you have to move into the guest room, it means something—it means somebody.

NORA
Well, if you knew, why the hell didn't you say something? Why didn't you *do* something?

OLIVER
Like what?

NORA
Like anything. My God, do you have to be told that, too? Like put your foot down, slam doors, belt me . . . walk out!

OLIVER
But that never seemed reasonable, or even consistent. After all, I knew when I married you that you were the girl who had to dance with everybody.

NORA
Bravo! Noël Coward would applaud. You're so civilized. You're so damned civilized you're practically inert!

OLIVER
(*Pursing his lips thoughtfully*)
You know, that's the second time somebody's said that to me today.

NORA

Why did you marry me? I mean honestly—really and truly—why?

OLIVER

Because your daddy was rich and you were good-lookin'.

NORA

You married me because it was the thing to do. Lots of people wanted to marry me in 1973. It just happened to be my year. Two of your friends proposed—so you proposed.

OLIVER

Ah, but I didn't propose! That was my whole attraction. I was the one who did not come rolling to your feet like a croquet ball. That was what was so special about me.

NORA

Are you saying you weren't in love with me?

OLIVER

Oh, I was in love with you—sick in love with you! But I didn't suppose I had a chance.

NORA
(Seizing on it)

Did you hear what you just said? That's what I mean. That was your attitude always: that you didn't have a chance!

OLIVER

Be that as it may, you did the proposing. Don't you remember? It was very romantic. We were at a party in Georgetown. It was very late and somebody put on Guy Lombardo playing "Three O'clock in the Morning." And everybody who wasn't too stoned was dancing. And then you discovered I couldn't dance. So you decided to teach me.

NORA

Oh, you could dance before that.

OLIVER

No, I couldn't. You taught me that night. And I bore you off in triumph in my old VW. Which broke down on Nineteenth Street. So we got out and started looking for a cab and all of a sudden it started to pour rain. It was a deluge, so we ran up the steps of what looked like a deserted brownstone. Anyway, there were no lights and we sat on what must have been an old window box. It's a wonder it didn't come crashing down. And I was becoming ardent, or as ardent as I could get with you in your mink coat and me in my ski jacket. Then out of the blue—well, out of the rain— you said, "You're much too uptight to ask me to live with you. So why don't we get married?"

NORA

I guess I did.

OLIVER

You know you did.

NORA

I don't remember that you put up much of a struggle.

OLIVER

No. I was very quick to pop the answer.

NORA
(*Weeping or close to it*)

This is shabby of you—really shabby! You want to know if it still hurts. Well, it does, dammit!

OLIVER

What does?

NORA

The memory of that night when everything was possible. When I thought you needed me.

OLIVER

I needed you.

NORA

You didn't. You don't. When do you listen to me? When do you even look at me?

OLIVER
(*Like a dagger*)

When are you *here*?

NORA
(*Letting fly*)

See, I'm guilty again! Always, always guilty! And you're the totally innocent victim! You honest-to-God think because you gave me your love and attention seven years ago, that's going to hold me forever!

OLIVER
(*Cutting her off sharply and going to the desk*)

Nora, you want to be soul-searching and Gothic. I just want to get some work done.
(*Sits to galleys*)

NORA

Dammit, even now you hide behind that book! You're so busy analyzing emotions—writing about them—you don't *have* emotions any more. Yours have dried up. You don't feel *anything*. You're dead.

OLIVER

Bullshit.

NORA

Now you're going to tell me you do feel something for her.

OLIVER

For who?

NORA

For *who?* That's perfect, that's absolutely perfect! Have you forgotten her name, or have you already forgotten her existence?

OLIVER

(He *has forgotten. In quick embarrassment* he *turns his head sharply away from* NORA)
Oh, oh, God—Mrs. Sachs.

NORA

Mrs. Sachs? Is it possible that you are not on a first-name basis?

OLIVER

(*Doing his best to square himself for it, moving away from the desk*)
All right. You're asking me a direct question. I'll give you an honest answer.

NORA

Please do.

OLIVER

I'm thinking about it. And the truth is yes . . . I *do* feel something
for Carrie.

NORA

You admit it? I'm surprised.

OLIVER
(*Short pause*)

You know something? You're not as surprised as I am.

(*And a brief silence as* NORA *absorbs this*)

Now that the air is alive with candor, you might tell me how you
feel about Peter Sachs.

NORA
(*After a split second's thought*)

I don't know. I'd like to find out.

OLIVER

Find out! Be my guest!

NORA

I have your permission—that's great! And you have that little teenager in her orthopedic sneakers! Well, you won't have me.
(*Snatching up her beach bag and beginning to cram
overnight things into it, which takes her off to the bedroom briefly*)

OLIVER

What are you doing?

NORA

I'm leaving. I'm clearing out.

OLIVER

You're what?

NORA

(*Returning, having also picked up a small, soft cosmetic bag*)

I'm going to leave the field open for you and your—your—your—

OLIVER

Chippie! I'd love it if you'd say "chippie"!

NORA

(*Throwing the cosmetic bag at him*)

Go to hell. And I must say I'm surprised that Leo would be a party to this.

(*Heads for the front door*)

OLIVER

Leo isn't a party to anything. They went to the New School together.

NORA

She went to school! I find that hard to believe. I think of her as a child of nature, picking up all her information from gray squirrels and buttercups.

OLIVER

Are you going for the evening—for the night—for the week?

NORA

I'm going for whatever damn well suits me! And you should get right down to that little book of yours. Maybe it's not too late to add a chapter. You've got a hell of a lot of new material.

(*Slamming the door as she leaves*)

OLIVER
(*Calling out*)

You keep in touch, hear?

(OLIVER *stares at the door for a second, turns on his heel, and heads for the desk, where he seats himself angrily and reaches for the galleys.*

Unfortunately, the sudden reach becomes a push, and he accidentally sends the galleys sliding forward off the desk and down into the fish tank, just beneath. OLIVER *rises, horror-stricken, to stare at what he has done*)

CURTAIN

ACT TWO

Scene One

Early that evening, not quite twilight. OLIVER *has an electric iron plugged into his desk, along with assorted towels and newspapers. He is pressing the galleys that got wet. He retrieves three galleys from the deck, where they have been drying. He picks up another from the fireplace screen and takes it to the desk, where he resumes ironing.* LEO *comes into the room through the deck doors, rather tentatively.*

LEO

Oliver?

OLIVER
(*Exactly duplicating* LEO's *tone*)

Leo?

LEO

Carrie's beginning to get nervous. She thinks she ought to go home. Do you want to see her before she goes?

OLIVER
(*A definite edge in his voice*)

Yes. Indeed. By all means.

LEO
(*Scenting trouble*)

Uh-oh!

(*Finally noticing the ironing*)

What are you doing?

OLIVER

You can see what I'm doing.

LEO

You're pressing newspapers. You see what a slob *I* am. I just throw mine out when they get wrinkled.

OLIVER

I am not pressing newspapers. I am drying the galleys of my book. They got wet.

LEO

Do you have to be so frantic about it?

OLIVER

Let me ask *you* a question. Do you think I'm too old to go to law school?

LEO

Stop ironing. That's woman's work. You're too frail. Sit down. Listen, my car is back now. So when Carrie is ready I'll drive her home. Just tell her to shake this bell. . . .

(He *picks up a small bell on a table near the deck entrance and gives it a* little *shake*)

I'll be out on my deck, so I'll hear it.

CARRIE

(*To* LEO *as she steals nervously onto deck from below*)

Is it all right?

LEO

He's all yours.
> (*Gives* CARRIE *a little salute as* he *leaves*)

OLIVER

> (*Looking at* CARRIE *and speaking in a mock-romantic tone*)

My darling! You *came* back! Oh me of little faith. I didn't trust you. I thought you'd never come. I thought—

CARRIE

Oh, you *are* furious, aren't you?

OLIVER

You're damn right I am.

CARRIE

It was a mistake to tell your wife that story.

OLIVER

You could say that. It was one of the great mistakes—
> (He *finally pauses to look at* CARRIE'*s new getup*)

And you went home and got all dressed up. What for?

CARRIE

Oh, no, I spilled port wine on my dress. You wouldn't believe how much wine there is in one glass. Look.
> (She *shows him her dress: red-blotched everywhere*)

Leo said I looked like Julius Caesar after the assassination. He let me borrow this dress of Melinda's.
> (*Nervous*)

I gather you and your wife had a quarrel. I heard her drive away.

OLIVER

What we had was worse than a quarrel. A quarrel is saying something in anger that you don't really mean. Nora meant what she said. We opened a door that always did have a rusty hinge. Who knows if we'll ever get it closed again.

CARRIE

Of course you will! I really am sorry. It was a terrible thing to do. I *heard* myself telling her this wild tale. I couldn't believe I was doing it.

OLIVER

You couldn't believe it!

CARRIE

You see, when she came in she was so great-looking and so—so in charge. I felt abandoned—out on this little ledge all by myself. I didn't think, I just jumped.

OLIVER

Pulling me with you.

CARRIE

That was the worst part. But why did you go along with it?

OLIVER

Because . . . I don't know. Maybe we all have little ledges . . . and I just noticed mine.

CARRIE

Listen, Oliver, there's nothing to be upset about. I'll go home and tell Peter I made up the whole thing. And he'll tell Nora.

OLIVER

That's what you will absolutely *not* do.

CARRIE

But why shouldn't I tell him that—

OLIVER

(*Interrupting quickly*)

Because if you pull at just one thread of this idiotic web you've woven . . . the whole thing will unravel. And we'll both look like fools.

CARRIE

Is that so terrible?

OLIVER

I happen to think so, yes. Besides, you will have stirred up a mess —and accomplished nothing. I presume you still want him back?

CARRIE

Of course I do.

OLIVER

Then you will go home and admit everything.

CARRIE

Wait a minute! Tell him that I had an affair with my Marriage Counselor! Isn't that awfully tacky?

OLIVER

It's very, *very* tacky! But you should have thought of that sooner.

CARRIE

Oh, he'll be very upset.

OLIVER

I expect so. He married you. He must care about you.

CARRIE

Well, I suppose, but that isn't what I mean. This is absolutely the worst time to be bothering him about things. His Jackson Pollack Retrospective opens at the Whitney on Monday.

OLIVER

You're telling me that Jackson Pollack is a lot more important to your husband . . . than you are.

CARRIE

You're putting it that way. Don't you like Jackson Pollack? Some people don't.

OLIVER

Carrie, how old are you?

CARRIE

Twenty-three.

OLIVER

It's time you knew who you were. You don't have to go on being The Little Match Girl.

CARRIE

I'm not. That's an awful thing to say.

OLIVER

But you are. And it's time to change that a little. Are you going to listen to me?

CARRIE

I'm listening.

OLIVER

All right. Now, you don't have to *tell* Peter anything. Nora will have called him.

CARRIE
(*Wailing*)

Oh no!

OLIVER

Stop that. Stop it right now. You're going home and you're going to appear composed. Don't deny anything. Don't be apologetic. Have you got a smile that doesn't look worried?

CARRIE

I never thought about it. I guess so.

OLIVER

Think of something surprising and marvelous. It doesn't have to be true. Think: I'm famous, my name turned up in the crossword puzzle today. Then smile. Let me see you do it.

(She *goes through the exercise and more or less succeeds*)

See, you look more grown-up already. Remember: Your attitude is simple. "These things happen." Say it.

CARRIE
(*Perplexed*)

"These things happen"?

OLIVER

There's no question mark at the end of that. You're reminding him of something he already knows. This is an exchange between adults. You're calm—cavalier, even.

(He's *eased her into an armchair to make her more relaxed, poised*)

CARRIE
(*Now saying it perfectly*)
Peter, these things happen—

OLIVER
Right!

CARRIE
(*Encouraged,* she *goes on improvising*)
They're like . . . thunderstorms in April. Sudden and unexpected. But they're not really dangerous, and they're over before you know it.

OLIVER
(*Stopping this*)
Fine. You've got it.

CARRIE
These storms—

OLIVER
I said you've got it. I promise you, he'll be impressed. Even if the whole truth comes out, he'll have to concede that you are far more complicated than he suspected.

CARRIE
Do you know, that's definitely existential. I'm becoming complicated in order to *seem* complicated.

OLIVER
It'll take me a while to figure that one out—but I think you've got it now. Good luck, Carrie.

CARRIE

Good-bye, Oliver, and thank you. You've really been so—so sterling.

OLIVER

'Bye. And don't grow up too much, okay? Just a little bit.

(CARRIE *grins and disappears onto deck. Twilight is beginning and there's a faint red glow in the sky.* OLIVER *looks after her reflectively a moment, then starts to his desk. Along the way, he spots something on the floor, picks it up. It is* CARRIE's *lighter. He flicks it a couple of times, smiling, then drops it into his pocket. Before he can get to the desk,* CARRIE *suddenly is back again*)

CARRIE

Oh, Oliver, I just thought! Listen, where is your office?

OLIVER

It's on Park Avenue, but why?

CARRIE

But where on Park Avenue? It's got to be near something, what's it near?

OLIVER

It's near Sixty-first Street. Why? Are you coming to see me?

CARRIE

Of course not. But I want to know what restaurant it's near—what hotels.

OLIVER

I don't understand.

CARRIE

I want to know where we went.

OLIVER

Where we went? We didn't go anywhere.

CARRIE

I know that, silly, but Peter will ask me where. And he'll know, of course, that we didn't—in your office. That *never* goes on in offices, does it?

OLIVER

There are exceptions—which have a way of getting into the newspapers—but in general it would be safe to say that it never happens in offices.

CARRIE

So where did we go—to a motel?

OLIVER

In Manhattan?

CARRIE

Yes, I suppose it would be a very long cab ride to find a real motel. But wouldn't it be a lot less embarrassing than going through a hotel lobby?

OLIVER

Of course, you don't have to go hand in hand through a hotel lobby—

CARRIE

That's right. *You* could get the key and go up to the room and then I could come up ten minutes later in a different elevator. But listen. We've skipped lunch.

OLIVER
(*Teasing her*)
That's all right. Some things are more important.

CARRIE
Don't joke. I'm trying to make this whole thing plausible. Concrete details are important. That's how I got your wife to believe that I had been your patient. I told her how I suffered under that gruesome painting of Saint Sebastian.

OLIVER
How on earth did you know that?

CARRIE
Leo told me.

OLIVER
He did? That boy lives dangerously.

CARRIE
Oh, he didn't know what I was going to do. But let's get back to the subject. We must have had lunch a couple of times before—before we—

OLIVER
Hit the sack? Maybe not. Maybe we were blind with passion. Food didn't matter.
(*Getting into the spirit of the thing*)
I'll tell you what we did. There's a luggage store around the corner. We go there, we buy a suitcase and we dump a couple of phone books in it. Then we go to some classy hotel like the St. Regis. And I say to the room clerk, "You have a reservation for Professor and Mrs. Roscoe Sommers?" And then, while he's checking, you say out loud, "Roscoe, did you check the rates?

This place seems very expensive to me." Nobody but a wife would say a dumb thing like that in a hotel lobby. So the clerk will come back and say, "I can't seem to find the reservation, but we do have a room, Professor."

CARRIE
(*Delighted*)

Oh, Oliver, that's neat. But look, I really and truly would have to have lunch first. What restaurants are near your office?

OLIVER

There are fifty restaurants.

CARRIE

But which one do you go to?

OLIVER

I don't go out to lunch. I have a Tab and a tuna salad sandwich sent up.

CARRIE

Oh, you're just trying to make trouble! Think. Surely there's some restaurant you've been to in that neighborhood.

OLIVER

Well, yes. Once in a while I have gone to a restaurant called Le Place.

CARRIE

The place?

OLIVER

Le Place. It's French.

CARRIE

That's bad French.

OLIVER

It's bad food, too.

CARRIE

Never mind the food. Do they have tables or booths?

OLIVER

They have a couple of tables in front, but mostly it's booths.

CARRIE

Good. That's why we go there.

(OLIVER *looks questioning*)

We'd want privacy.

OLIVER

It's not *that* private. I say we go to a hotel.

CARRIE

Oliver, please take this seriously. I've got to face Peter and I've got to get my story straight. There's still one real gap that bothers me.

OLIVER

What's that?

CARRIE

I can see how it would be easy to have lunch the second time. But the first time would be really peculiar—I mean, for a doctor to suggest such a thing. I go to see you. The hour is up and you say, "On your way out, Miss Jones will give you an appointment for next week—and by the way, how about lunch on Tuesday?" See, that's impossible. It just wouldn't happen.

OLIVER

Not *that* way, certainly.

CARRIE
(*Grabbing his hands in excitement*)
Oliver, I've got it! It's simple as pie. I'm inspired!

OLIVER
(*Grinning at her*)
All right, tell me.

CARRIE

When's your lunch break?

OLIVER

One to two.

CARRIE

Okay, I have the appointment right before lunch. Twelve to one, right?

OLIVER
(*Nodding*)
Twelve to one.

CARRIE

And I'm on my diet. I'm always on a diet. And I get faint and dizzy like I did today. And you're sort of concerned about me. And that's why you take me to lunch.

OLIVER

Why don't I send for a sandwich from the deli?

CARRIE

It's a Jewish holiday. The delicatessen is closed.

OLIVER

It's not a Jewish delicatessen.

CARRIE
(*Indignant*)
Are you trying to get out of this?

OLIVER
(*Emphatically*)
Never!

CARRIE

Then stop creating problems. Anyway, the first lunch was entirely innocent.

OLIVER
(*Waggling his eyebrows*)
Ah, but the *second* lunch!

CARRIE

What are you doing with your eyebrows?

OLIVER

I'm trying to leer.

CARRIE

Well, don't.
(*Back to her story*)

In the second lunch, you gradually overcome my objections. Listen, how do you do that?

OLIVER

I tell you about my loneliness, my needs—my feeling that I can't relate to anybody—

CARRIE
(*Shaking her head*)
I must tell you: That sounds awfully boring to me.

OLIVER

Look, dummy, it's not a panel discussion. You don't have to have a topic. You can talk about *anything*.

CARRIE

Like what?

OLIVER

You're really hopeless. Look, we'll say this is a booth—
　　(*Indicates small settee just downstage of counter at Right*)
This is the table—
　　　　(He *pulls a table in front of settee*)
And this is the other bench.
　　(*Picks up coffee table and places it facing settee across table*)
You sit here.
　　(*Points to settee, and* she *hesitantly sits on upstage side, leaving no space for him*)
Now, you slide over—indicating that I should sit beside you.

　　(She *moves hastily to make room*)

You don't lunge! You just ease over—the least little bit—

(She *does this almost too invitingly, but* OLIVER *surprisingly reverses field and goes to sit on bench facing her. The twilight outside is deepening, the sky glowing a bright orange*)

CARRIE

Aren't you going to sit here?

OLIVER

No. I want to be able to look at you.

(CARRIE *jumps up*)

Where are you going?

CARRIE

I'm nervous. I've got to have a cigarette.
   (She *rummages in her large bag, fishes out a crumpled pack of cigarettes and sits down again*)
I'm back.

OLIVER

I see.

CARRIE

Oh, dear, I've lost my lighter again. Do you have any matches?

OLIVER
   (*Reaching into his pocket*)
I have your lighter.

CARRIE

Oh, thank you. It's so dumb the way I keep dropping it.
   (She *reaches for the lighter, but* OLIVER *doesn't let go. There is a small struggle for it*)

OLIVER

I'll light it.

CARRIE

I can light it.

OLIVER

I know you can light it. But you're going to let *me* light it.

CARRIE

(*Very sagely getting the point and relaxing her grip*)
Oh.

(OLIVER *lights it, holding onto her hand for a bit*)

OLIVER

I wish I could get you to stop smoking.

CARRIE

Why?

OLIVER

Because it's bad for you. Because I don't want to lose you.

CARRIE

Is that part of the script or are you really talking to me?

OLIVER

Fifty-fifty. Stop making remarks about the script or you'll never get anywhere. You'll never learn anything.

CARRIE

You're right. I should stay in character.

OLIVER

Remember, we're in the last booth. And the place is almost empty.
There is just one waiter left, and he's old and half blind and deaf.
Anyway, he's up front setting up the tables for dinner.

CARRIE

It does feel like we're alone, doesn't it?

OLIVER

I felt we were alone in all the traffic on Sixty-first Street. I didn't
notice anybody else, did you?

CARRIE

No, I didn't.
(*Nervous again*)
Well, I guess we should order.

OLIVER

There's no hurry. We have all the time in the world.

(She *starts to look at her watch.* OLIVER *puts his hand
on her wrist, covering the watch and leaving his hand
there*)

You're not supposed to look at your watch. You're supposed to
look at me. Think of all the days I won't be able to see you. Hundreds of them.

CARRIE
(*Gulping*)
Yeah.

(OLIVER *moves over to the settee, close beside her*)

OLIVER

That's a pretty locket. I never noticed it before.

CARRIE

It belonged to my mother. Dad gave it to her when they got married.

OLIVER

Does it open?

CARRIE

Oh, yes.
    (She *opens the locket and leans forward so that* he *can see it*)
The picture is sort of fading. That's my dad when he was in the Navy.

OLIVER
(*Holding onto the locket*)

I see.

CARRIE

But you're not looking at it.

OLIVER

Carrie, I didn't really want to see the locket. I wanted you to come a little closer.

CARRIE

Oliver, I think maybe I want to stop this.

OLIVER

Why? What are you afraid of?

CARRIE

Don't be silly—I'm not afraid.

OLIVER

But you are. There's a little blue vein right there.

(He *touches her neck*)

I can see it pulsing. And you're pale. I can see little golden freckles.

CARRIE

I always have freckles. I put stuff on—so you don't notice.

OLIVER

You shouldn't. They're very interesting freckles. Have you ever been to Paris?

CARRIE

No, I've never been to anything. I've just been in the United States.

OLIVER

Well, in the Jeu des Paumes—that's a small gallery that's part of the Louvre—there's a Monet painting of a girl with a parasol. She's standing on a little hill. And you can tell from the light that the day is perfect. And you can tell from her expression that she is expecting somebody wonderful. Her happiness is so tangible. I've seen the painting a dozen times and every time I see it, I have the same feeling: "This is the way life is supposed to be. Whatever happened?" Anyway, you remind me of that girl in the painting—so wide-eyed and so expectant. I just wish that—

CARRIE

(*Picking up the thread*)

You wish that I was happy, like the girl in the painting.

OLIVER

Yes, that's what I wish.

CARRIE

But, see, that's just one moment. We don't know what happened. Maybe she waited and waited. And it started to rain. And then she had to walk down the hill all alone.

OLIVER

Carrie . . . whatever happens, I really don't want you to have to walk down the hill alone. Do you hear me?

CARRIE
(*Touching his cheek with her hand*)
Oliver, you really are very sweet. Don't worry about me. I'm used to walking down hills alone.

OLIVER

Well, you shouldn't be. Look—he's gone!

CARRIE

Who? Who's gone?

OLIVER

The waiter. He's gone into the kitchen . . .

(She *turns her head away as though to see the waiter. As* she *is turning back,* OLIVER *is ready for her*)

Quick! Kiss me.

(He *cups her face in his hands and kisses her soundly*)

CARRIE
(*Amazed and delighted*)
Oliver, you're so *good* at this!

OLIVER

Okay—again. It's like learning a new word. You have to use it three times before it's yours.

(*There's one light kiss, followed by a longer one*)

CARRIE

I guess we should order now.

OLIVER
(*Standing up suddenly*)

I'm not hungry.

CARRIE

Neither am I.
(She *stands up too*)
We'll just leave five dollars for the waiter because we mussed up his table.

OLIVER

All right. Would you be willing to buy a suitcase now?

CARRIE
(*Reflectively, then a slight smile*)

No, I guess I wouldn't. But Oliver—

OLIVER

Yes?

CARRIE

I would really and truly love to have lunch again.

OLIVER
(*Laughing*)

Carrie, you're twelve years old and I don't want you to turn thirteen!

(He *puts his arms out and* she *steps into them. He kisses her again*)

CARRIE

What's that for?

OLIVER

The hell of it.
(*Suddenly exuberant*)
Come on, never mind suitcases—we're going to take a swim!

CARRIE

At this hour?

OLIVER

Sure! Don't you ever do anything spontaneously?

CARRIE

But I don't have a bathing suit—oh, of course I do!
(*Fishing one out of her large bag*)

OLIVER

I'll get mine.

(He *goes into the bedroom area. Having found hers,* CARRIE *moves somewhat apprehensively to the deck windows, peering out and down, shading her eyes from the reflection*)

CARRIE
(*Calling back to him*)
Oliver—! It's awful dark down there!

(110)

OLIVER (Off)
(*From bedroom*)

There are lights all the way down! The switch is right there by the curtains.

(CARRIE *immediately pulls the draperies aside to reveal a small bank of switches. She turns one on and gets a great blare of Tchaikovsky's* "Romeo and Juliet Overture")

CARRIE
(*Startled, lets out a bleat*)

Oliver! Hey, what did I do?

OLIVER
(*Reappearing rapidly from bedroom, carrying his swimming trunks*)

You turned on the tape deck. Leo's got it wired so it will play all over the house—and down on the float.

(OLIVER *lowers the volume. It's darker now, with only the last traces of twilight lingering*)

CARRIE

Listen, what about towels?

OLIVER

There's a locker on the lower deck with towels.

(As CARRIE *and* OLIVER *move onto the deck,* they *nearly bump into* LEO, *who's been waiting to be summoned and has just run up the deck stairs*)

LEO

I was waiting for one bell—not the Philharmonic.
(*Sees the bathing suits they're carrying*)

Now what?

CARRIE

Leo, I'm not going home yet. I'm going swimming.

LEO

With him? He can't swim; you'll drown.

OLIVER

You think I can't swim because you've never seen me swim. I was
a lifeguard for two years at Revere Beach.

(*Phone rings*)

Leo, get it, will you?

LEO

What if it's Nora?
          (*Reluctantly going toward phone*)
What'll I tell her?

OLIVER

          (*Calling over the music from the deck*)
You will tell her the truth.

LEO

The truth? That you've gone swimming? Oh, I'd be careful. Nora's
a very confused woman *now*.

OLIVER

It's your opportunity, Leo. Tell her what's in your heart!

(OLIVER *and* CARRIE *disappear into the dark. Phone has
continued ringing, and* LEO *picks it up, immediately assuming a flat, metallic voice*)

LEO
(*Into phone*)

This . . . is a recording—

(*The music swells again*)

CURTAIN

(*Music continues until curtain rises on following scene*)

ACT TWO

Scene Two

Half an hour later. The room is dark except for the little light that illuminates the fish tank. There is bright moonlight outside, however, so that we can see that it's a man who lets himself in by the front door. He tiptoes across the room with the stem of a pair of eyeglasses clenched between his teeth. It is, of course, PETER SACHS, *and he begins bumping into the furniture as he calls out:*

PETER

Carrie! . . . CARRIE! DeVreck! . . . ANYBODY!
     (He *pushes open a couple of doors, still calling*)
Hello, there! . . . Yoo-hoo!
     (He *goes back to the front door and calls out to* NORA)
Nora. NORA! Please don't stand there. Your buddy in the basement was correct. It's totally empty.
     (*As* NORA *enters*)
Nora, why are we creeping in here like commandos? You live here. We're not going to be arrested for breaking and entering.

NORA

That's not the point.
     (NORA *begins snapping on lights, tentatively and apprehensively*)

PETER

Darling girl, what is the point?

NORA

Peter, don't you understand? It's just two hours since I made my farewell speech and slammed out of here. The windows are still rattling. I absolutely do not, do NOT want to run into Oliver.

PETER

Why not? He doesn't bite. I gather he doesn't do much of anything. Listen, you came back here to pack. Come on! Pack.

NORA
(*Throwing her arms around him*)
Oh, Peter, do I know what I'm doing?

PETER

Well, right now you're holding on to me, which I thoroughly approve of, but it won't get the packing done. And you're the one who's trying to avoid your husband. I'm perfectly willing to talk to him. I'd *like* to talk to him.

NORA

Never! Peter, you do not grasp. Something happened today—like maybe my whole life blew up.

PETER

You're exaggerating.

NORA

No, I told Oliver the truth about us. And worse, oh much worse, I told him the truth about *him*. I broke something. It may not be possible to repair it. Maybe I don't want to repair it. But I want to feel you understand. I want to feel you're there.

PETER

There? I'm here, right here.

(*Saluting*)

Present, ma'am.

(He *kisses her*)

NORA

I know, I know—I'm just nervous. And where do you suppose they are? They haven't got a car.

PETER

Come on, you're not going to accomplish anything standing there tapping your foot.

NORA

I'm thinking.

PETER

Look, I'll think. You pack. Move. Put one foot in front of the other.

NORA

Watch me, I'm moving.

(NORA *disappears into the bedroom, still talking*)

The suitcase is in here. It's *got* to be in here.

PETER

(*Calling out to her as* he *wanders about the room, get-ting a look at it*)

While you're packing—do you have a simple basic black?

NORA (Off)

Sure!

PETER

Don't bring it! I hate basic black.

> (He's *arrived at the doors to the deck, we see him sud-*
> *denly become alert, peering out intently and calling to*
> NORA)

Hey, Nora! There's somebody out there swimming!

NORA (Off)

Well, it's not Oliver.

PETER

It might even be two people. Come here and look.

NORA

> (*Returning with suitcase*)

I don't have to look. If it's swimming, it's not Oliver. Do you know what really burns me up?

PETER

Me.

> (He *leans over and kisses her*)

NORA

> (*Pulls out of the kiss and continues*)

Oliver is going to think I left because I'm jealous.

PETER

Nora, he did not expect you to believe Carrie's wild story.

NORA

I think he did. *He* was going along with it. Do you know something? If I thought he was actually having an affair, I'd celebrate. I think.

PETER
(*Wryly*)

Think again.

NORA

But really, it would be quite marvelous to see him take his first
baby step in the direction of something human. . . .

PETER

Well, if he ever does take a little plunge, I promise you it's not
going to be with Carrie.

NORA

You're sure?

PETER

My God, Nora, you've met her. She's a hopeless, helpless child.

NORA

Oh? Then why did you marry her?

PETER

I don't know. Maybe because she *was* so hopeless. And then, she
was so sweet with Nancy.

NORA

Your daughter?

PETER

(He *nods yes, but as the speech goes on* he *becomes*
quite heated)

And for that matter, she was sweet with me. Everyone said she
was like a breath of spring. And she *was* like a breath of spring.
But sooner or later, the best spring in the world has by God got

to be summer! I shouldn't have married her, I should have adopted her.

NORA
(*Pursing her lips, shrewdly*)
You know, I have met this little lady. She doesn't seem all that retarded to me.

PETER
(*Palms up in exasperation*)
Nora! She still keeps her bobby pins in an eggcup.
(*Shooing her back to suitcase*)
Come on! Finish packing. And whatever you do, don't forget your passport.

NORA
My passport?
(*Alerted and uneasy*)
Peter, I thought you made a reservation at the Hampstead.

PETER
Well, for tonight, yes. But you didn't think we were going to *stay* there! Darling girl, we said we were going away together. The Hampstead isn't away, it's two miles from here.

NORA
I know, but we need more time to think, Peter, we don't want to be really rash.

PETER
Speak for yourself. I want to be rash, very, very rash. All the men in my family become conservative early. Any minute now I'll turn into my father. Nora, you can save me. Listen, I'll make love to you all the way to Venezuela.

NORA

Venezuela?

PETER

We're going to Bunny's place.

NORA

Who's Bunny?

PETER

Bunny Richards. He's got this huge ranch in Venezuela—and listen, if I ask Binx Ryan, I'm sure he'll lend us his jet.

NORA

Peter, don't you know any ordinary people—any *poor* people?

PETER

Poor people with their own jet? No. Nora, what's the matter? Don't you like me any more?

NORA

Oh, Peter, what a question!

PETER
(*Serious*)

Darling, you've got to decide. This afternoon I met you—at the time you set. My heart was making so much noise I thought the kid that parked my car was going to hear it. Then you arrive. And after just one minute you say you have to call home about your electric blanket. And the next thing, you're dashing off because Oliver "sounded peculiar." And I'm left there by myself, like a crazy person. Then—

NORA
(*Putting up her hand to stop him*)

I remember!

PETER

Then—an hour ago you call and say: "Peter, I'm ready. Let's do it. Let's go."

(*Demanding*)

Well, are we going to *go?*

NORA
(*Throwing open her arms*)

Oh, darling, sure we are!

(NORA *and* PETER *are embracing ardently downstage as* OLIVER *and* CARRIE *appear on the deck, happily, hand in hand. They see* NORA *and* PETER *kiss, quickly look at each other. Immediately* CARRIE *puts out her arms to* OLIVER, *and he picks her up in his arms. Since she is wearing an oversize terrycloth bathrobe, it's quite a sight.* OLIVER *and* CARRIE *kiss—and hold it until somebody notices them*)

PETER
(*The first to become aware of the situation and pulling out of his kiss with* NORA)

Nora—

NORA
(*Dreamily, unaware*)

What?

(*Looks and sees*)

Oh, my God!

CARRIE
(*Cheerily*)

Oh, hi.

PETER
(*In a tense whisper*)

Nora, introduce us.

NORA
(*Also tense and hissing*)

No, it's too *dumb*.

PETER

Nora, *say* something!

NORA

I won't.

PETER
(*Sharply but still whispering*)

Intro*duce* us!

OLIVER
(*To* CARRIE)

Hey, wasn't that moon something!
(*To* PETER, *agreeably—but focusing on* CARRIE)

I'm Oliver.

CARRIE

The moon *and* the water. *Everything!*

OLIVER
(*To* CARRIE)

And how is that foot—all right?

CARRIE

(*To* OLIVER, *ignoring the others*)

It was just a broken clamshell. I *told* you it was nothing. You know salt water is a natural disinfectant.

OLIVER

Yes, Doctor.

CARRIE

It must have been tough carrying me up those stairs.

(*Lightly touching his chest*)

Your heart is pounding.

OLIVER

It is. I noticed. What makes you think it's from the stairs?

CARRIE

(*Slipping down from his arms and saying playfully*)

Oliver!

(*New thought*)

You know, I've been skinny for two years. And this is the first time I got any use out of it.

OLIVER

That's hard to believe.

CARRIE

No, honestly.

(NORA *and* PETER, *who have been listening with increasing exasperation, speak together*)

PETER

Carrie, are you stoned or something?

(*Together*)

NORA

Is this little duet going to go on forever?

OLIVER

(*Putting his hands over his ears*)

Wait, wait, wait! If you'll just speak one at a time, I'll be happy to answer all questions.

(*Judicially, like a schoolteacher*)

Now, who was first?

NORA

(*Icily*)

I would like to know why you are making this elaborate pretense that Peter and I are not here?

OLIVER

(*Fake sheepish*)

I'm afraid you kind of caught us by surprise.

CARRIE

(*Going over to* PETER)

Oh, Peter, you know it's really special to swim when there's just a slice of moon. Like tonight. When you walk out on the dock, the water looks so cold and hard—like a great big pan of fudge. But when you dive into it—it's so soft and warm.

PETER

You're not really going to give me a disquisition on the glories of moonlight bathing?

CARRIE
(*Pleased*)

You're irritated with me. Hey, that's a step! You haven't noticed me in months.

PETER

Carrie, try to make sense.

CARRIE
(*Going into her prepared speech*)

Don't be upset. These things happen. They're like thunderstorms in April, sudden and unexpected. But they're not dangerous and they're over before you know it—

PETER

It's *not* April, there are no storms. What the hell are you talking about?

CARRIE

Oliver, did I say that wrong?

OLIVER

No, I think your husband just chooses not to understand.

NORA
(*To* OLIVER)

And YOU, who will not go swimming in the middle of the day when the sun is shining, can suddenly find the time and the strength at this hour—when if *I* ever—

OLIVER
(*Lifting one hand*)

PLEASE! Before this breaks down into a series of little squabbles, I'd like to explain our plan.

NORA

Your *plan?*

PETER

(Switching gears and realizing that it's time for him to come to grips with the situation)

Wait a minute, Nora. He wants to be adult. I'm *with* him. Shoot, fella.

NORA

Fella?

(Collapsing onto settee)

Oh, my God!

OLIVER

Nora, please! What we have here is a simple problem in logistics. Carrie and I want to be together. Nora and Mr. Sachs—

(Interrupting himself)

And why don't I say Peter? Since we're getting so cozy. Nora and Peter want to be together. And the only thing that is keeping us all apart—*and* unhappy—is the lack of a coherent idea. So let me get right to the point. Peter, how do you feel about this house?

PETER

That's the point? What difference does it make how I feel about this house?

OLIVER

Well, I think it's important that you have a "right" feeling about it. Nora, why don't you show him around?

(To PETER, *like a good salesman)*

The kitchen is small, but there is a dishwasher.

(To NORA)

And don't forget to show him the little deck off the master bedroom.

(To PETER *again)*

It's really very charming and it gets the morning sun.

(To everybody)

And now I have to call my secretary.

(OLIVER *goes to the phone and dials*)

PETER

What's he talking about?

NORA

I haven't any idea.

OLIVER

(On the phone)

Helen? Are you just dashing out the door? Good. Listen. Would you try to get me two seats on the eight o'clock flight to Paris tomorrow night. Yeah. And cable the Meurice. I want that suite that looks over the Tuileries. One of the old ones. With a chandelier and large, hunky sofas. That's right—early Vanderbilt. Bless you.

(OLIVER *hangs up and turns to* PETER, *who hasn't moved*)

You *don't* want to see the rest of the place, I guess. I understand. As long as Nora is here beside you, the wilderness were paradise enow.

NORA

(Crossly, the first sign of real concern)

You're waiting for me to ask you what this means. Well, I won't.

OLIVER

(Breezily ignoring NORA; *strides to his desk, picking up galleys)*

I'll have to mail these back to Doubleday. They'll scream blue murder—what the hell, let them!

PETER

All right, Nora, if you won't ask, I will. What *are* you rambling on about?

OLIVER

Rambling? I thought I was being very direct. Carrie and I are going to Paris for the month of July. I'd like to take the first week in August also—but that may not be possible.
(*He opens his arms to* CARRIE *and she runs right into them for a hug*)

PETER
(*Unbelieving*)

Carrie is going to Paris!

NORA

You two are going to Paris?

CARRIE
(*In control now*)

Isn't that something? Oliver couldn't believe that I've never been to Paris, never seen the Louvre.

OLIVER

Ah, and you never had dinner at Le Grand Vefours! If we bribe the waiter, he'll give us the table where Colette used to sit. . . .

CARRIE

And we'll never have to order french fried potatoes. They'll just come that way!
(*Indicating to* OLIVER *that* NORA *and* PETER *are staring*)
Oliver, we're being inconsiderate. *Our* plans are set. But that leaves Peter and Nora kind of up in the air.

OLIVER

If Peter will just listen, I'm getting to that—

(*To* PETER)

Now, the rent on this house is paid for through Labor Day. And Nora, of course, has always liked it here. That's why I keep asking you, Peter, do *you* like it?

PETER

You are seriously suggesting that I move in here—while you take my wife out of the country?
 (*With a burst of irritated but actual concern, turning to* CARRIE)
Are you actually, literally planning to go someplace with this character? My God, Carrie, you don't even *know* him!

NORA

The hell she doesn't!
 (*To* PETER)
You're a quick-change artist! We're all set to go out the door to Bunny and Binxie's, and now you want to check references! And is that your main concern—does she *know* him?!

PETER
 (*To* NORA)
Well, Nora, it's a fair-enough question. Aren't *you* curious?

NORA
 (*Furious*)
No, as a matter of actual fact, I am *not* curious. I'm not the least tiny *bit* curious!
 (She *bursts out of the room, followed immediately by* PETER)

PETER
 (*As* he *goes into the bedroom after* NORA)
Nora, darling. Don't be like that. Be Nora!

NORA (Off)

What's Nora?

PETER (Off)
(*Conciliating*)

Nora's marvelous and she's *grown-up!* And she's not the girl I'm crazy about, she's the girl I'm sane about.

(OLIVER *and* CARRIE *have been listening, but* OLIVER *now shuts the bedroom door firmly, cutting the voices out*)

OLIVER

Carrie . . . I think it's going to work.

CARRIE

I think so too. I think they're coming to their senses. Oliver, you're a genius.

OLIVER
(*Wrapping his arms about her for a triumphant hug*)

I know.

CARRIE

Listen, I've got to get dressed. Where'll I go?

OLIVER
(*Pointing*)

The bathroom.

CARRIE

No, I don't want to be where I can hear them talking. I'll slip in here.

(*Indicating the breakfast nook. She picks up her bag and Melinda's dress and goes into the breakfast area*)

I'll only be a second. Don't look! I really am a quick dresser.

OLIVER
(*Standing with his back to* CARRIE)

Carrie?

CARRIE
(*From time to time maybe we see her head*)

Yeah? I'm listening.

OLIVER

You know, this is pretty bizarre behavior for a professional marriage counselor.

CARRIE

Well, yes, I suppose it is.

OLIVER

You *suppose!* I assure you this will be a landmark case.

CARRIE

What's that old saying? Desperate remedies require desperate diseases.

OLIVER

You've got it backwards. It's desperate *diseases* require desperate remedies.

CARRIE

That's me. I get everything backwards.

OLIVER
(*New tone. He's been thinking about* CARRIE *and their time down on the beach*)

Not everything. Something has happened, Carrie. All of a sudden I don't know whether I have the stomach to go on with this.

CARRIE

But you have to. Please. We have our two marriages to consider.

OLIVER

And we have something else to consider, don't we?

CARRIE
(*Reappearing*)

What?

OLIVER

You and me.

CARRIE

(*Going to him and clenching her fingers into his clenched fingers*)

Oliver, I don't know what's with me. I feel funny—like I couldn't swallow. I really feel convalescent, like I was just waking up in the recovery room and I know they were supposed to *do* something. And I'm trying to remember if it was serious.

OLIVER

What if it *is* serious?

CARRIE

Yeah, what will the robin do then, poor thing?

OLIVER

That's what I'm asking.

CARRIE

Oliver, you have to believe me, I can't think at all. I've only known you a couple of hours and I've known Peter three years. You've got to handle this.

OLIVER

All right, I will. I'll handle it.

> (OLIVER *picks up the cowbell and gives it a rousing shake*)

CARRIE
(Startled)

Oliver!

PETER

> (*Summoned, as it were, by the bell.* He *is followed by* NORA)

My God! What's that?

NORA
(*To* OLIVER)

You're calling Leo. We don't want Leo up here.

OLIVER

But we do. We've got to work out all the details.

PETER

> (*Finally noticing* CARRIE *in the new dress*)

What have *you* got on?

CARRIE

It's Melinda's dress. Do you like it?

PETER

Who's Melinda?

NORA
(Exasperated)

Who's Melinda?!! Who the hell cares about Melinda!

LEO
(*Entering*)

I care deeply. But she's gone.

CARRIE
(*Formal introductions*)

Leo Simpson, this is my husband, Peter.

OLIVER
(*Overriding the amenities*)

Leo, you had dinner with Carrie. So I suppose you know something of our situation?

LEO

Yes, I plied her with fine wine and got most of the story. I found it enthralling.

OLIVER

There are little gaps here and there. But we're working it out.

LEO

Thank God you called me. I have the solution.

NORA

Oh, Leo, *really*.

CARRIE
(*Jumping in*)

What is your idea, Leo? I'd like to know.

(*The others glare*)

Well, an outsider can be more objective.

LEO

Exactly. I can view this in its historical perspective. Twenty years ago the solution would have been simple. Carrie would return to Peter, and Nora would remain with Oliver. Convention would demand it. *Ten* years ago, they would just have switched partners —wife swapping. Convention would have demanded it. But now we've moved into the eighties. What we're looking for is a new way to solve an old problem. That's why I suggest a lottery.

PETER

A *what?*

LEO

(Pronouncing every syllable and starting to tear strips of paper, dropping them into a basket)

Lot-ter-y. Rhymes with pottery. You place all your names in the basket. Who you pick is who you get.

OLIVER, NORA, CARRIE
(In unison)

Leo!

LEO

Oh, and I'll put my name in too. It will add spice.

OLIVER

You mean I could end up with *you?*

LEO

That's a flaw in your character, Oliver. You have a problem for every solution.

OLIVER

Now *can* we get down to business!

PETER
(*Getting up to leave*)

Nora, I make it a point to leave parties when the games begin. I'm going. Will you come with me?

NORA

With you AND your wife? Or are you planning to leave her here?

CARRIE

You see, we *do* have a problem of logistics.

OLIVER

And that's why I wanted Leo. If we are going to sublet this house to Peter, we really have to have Leo's permission. Now, this would be somewhat different, and of course Nora would be here. But I think we should ask Leo if he has any stipulations, any questions.

LEO

I certainly do. First of all, Sachs, are you good with plants?

PETER
(*Turning to* NORA *in exasperation*)

Nora, really and truly I cannot—

LEO
(*Interrupting*)

There's no use appealing to Nora. She took care of them the first summer. It was a disaster. She overwatered them. That's what your amateur does. The rabbit fern turned yellow. The dracena got root rot. By Labor Day I had seven very sick plants on my hands.

NORA

Leo, you honestly think this is the moment to be talking about your lousy, rotten plants?

LEO

Nora, I'm shocked. You're living a lie. What were you *really* thinking when you helped me carry the grape ivy to the nursery to be repotted?

NORA

You should be repotted.

LEO

And no long-haired dogs. I have a very powerful vacuum cleaner. But you can't get those hairs.

(PETER *and* NORA *are gradually being overwhelmed by the barrage*)

CARRIE
(*To* NORA)

By the way, Mrs. DeVreck, Peter eats the same thing for breakfast every day. All-Bran mixed with Dutch-apple yogurt. He'll take wild cherry if he has to, but he prefers Dutch-apple.

OLIVER

And speaking of breakfast, Peter, I would advise you not to talk to Nora before, or during, breakfast.

NORA
(*Furious*)

Oliver, stop this! Stop it right now! I will not, not have it! How dare you presume to dispose of me as though I were chattel!

OLIVER

Chattel? I haven't heard that word in a long time. No one is disposing of you. Carrie and I are accommodating ourselves to what is an already existing relationship. If you're upset, it's because you think we're going to have *fun*.

NORA

You think this is a responsible attitude?

OLIVER

No, I think it's totally irresponsible! That's what I like about it.

CARRIE
(*Sharing his mood, but meaning it*)

Oliver and I . . . need something to regret.

PETER
(*To* CARRIE, *sharply*)

What you need is to go home and lie down. You're way out of your depth here.
(*Seizing* CARRIE *by the wrist and hustling her toward front door*)

I'm taking you out of this.
(*Stops to turn back to* NORA)

I'll come for you tomorrow.

OLIVER
(*Enraged*)

Oh, buddy, you're a peach! First you're going to take *your* wife, then you're going to come back and get *my* wife. Are you sure that's enough? Listen, there's a girl down the road who's a knockout, maybe you ought to check her out! Maybe you ought to—

PETER
(*Interrupting*)
Look, I don't have to take any more crap from you.

OLIVER
Oh, but you *do!*

PETER
And you're a marriage counselor! What you don't seem to grasp is that your profession is already something of a joke. Every therapist I ever met was an idiot. But they aren't in *your* class. You're gunning for the title.

OLIVER
Be that as it may. I work for a living. I perform services for which I am paid. And, once in a while, once in a great while, I'm worth it. What about you, Mr. Moneybags? You collect paintings, you collect women—and you've got a great tan—but you don't do anything!

PETER
On the other hand, when I wanted to get married I was able to propose to my wife, which, I understand, is more than you were able to do.

NORA
(*Dismayed, embarrassed*)
Oh, Peter—

LEO
(*Putting his hand on* NORA's *arm*)
Nora, you're way out of your depth here. Come on, get your things. I'm taking you out of this.

PETER
(*Shoving* LEO *so* he *spins away from* NORA)
Take your hands off her!

OLIVER
(*To* PETER)
Who are *you* to tell him to take his hands off her? I'll tell him to
take his hands off her—
(*Quickly, to* LEO)
Leo, you can put your hands on her.
(*Wheeling back to* PETER)
And as for you, chump—

PETER
(*Cool, approaching* OLIVER *on the level above the sofa*)
Would you like to step outside?

OLIVER
Good idea! We can throw sand at each other.

PETER
Sand, hell! I'll—
(He *throws a wild punch at* OLIVER. OLIVER *ducks and*
PETER *teeters forward, tumbling down over the back of
the sofa onto the sofa itself, and then bouncing onto the
floor.* CARRIE *instantly runs to him*)

CARRIE
Don't you touch him!
(*In her plunge forward,* she *lands on* PETER *with a
thump, quickly cries out as* he *groans*)
I'm sorry! Are you all right? Did you break anything?

PETER
(To CARRIE—*and curiously deflated)*

I didn't break anything. I never break anything—

(He *lifts himself to a sitting position, back against the sofa*)

—you know that. I lead a charmed life. That's because I'm so rich. Actually, it's surprising that I even fell down. The laws of gravity don't apply to me.

CARRIE
(Disturbed)

What are you talking about?

PETER

I'm talking about the privileges of the very rich.
(To OLIVER)

You say I don't do anything. Know something? You're absolutely correct. I'm sure you keep case histories. You might be interested to know what it's like to inherit nine million dollars when you're twenty-one—and you haven't finished college yet. It's a bitch. For the record—it's very hard to do something if you don't . . . *need* . . . the money. It takes a lot of character. I haven't got a lot of character.

CARRIE

Peter, you do have character.

PETER

No, I have money and I've always been good-looking. That's why you never noticed.

(He*'s getting up now and his tone is brisker. To* CARRIE)

I'm not wistful about it, you understand. There is this to be said about having money. You get rejected by a higher class of people.

(*Pats* CARRIE *on the head, almost as* OLIVER *did earlier*)

OLIVER

You know, Sachs, you're going to be harder to deal with if you turn out to be an actual human being.

NORA

You don't have to deal with him.

OLIVER
(*To* NORA—*very sharply*)
Look, we're all in a nice, fat mess which you stirred up. And *somebody* has to deal with it.

NORA
(*Mad*)
All *right! I'll* deal with it. So—everybody! All of you—OUT!

(They *look at her, stunned*)

And that includes Oliver—out of my house. This minute!

LEO

Your house?

NORA
(*More calmly, but definitely*)
You may own the house, Leo. But I have leased it for the summer. That's right, Oliver. The lease is in my name. I signed it. I always sign it. That's another of the things you're too busy to do. I'll pack your suitcase and leave it on the deck. You can pick it up any old time.
(*To the others*)
I've already lost my manners. I don't want to lose my temper. So would you—please—be good enough to leave? This party is over.
(She *slams herself into chair at* OLIVER's *desk, with finality. To fill the void,* LEO *promptly assumes the tones of a shipboard games master urging his flock on*)

LEO

The next party begins immediately, one floor below!
> (*Going up to tape deck, reaching for the switch that controls the music*)

All those wishing to say bon voyage to our departing couple Carrie and Oliver will join me in a farewell toast. I have a bottle of champagne and a large bag of Fritos! And the first one down gets to swing in the hammock.
> (He *pushes tape deck button to start Guy Lombardo's "Three O'clock in the Morning" and makes a move as though to lead the party downstairs but is checked by* NORA's *outburst*)

NORA
(On the edge of tears)

Damn you, Leo! Damn you. You never know when to stop. You never know when enough is enough. You've got to be funny—no matter what's falling apart.
> (She *collapses forward onto the desk and we detect real tears*)

No matter *who's* falling apart.

> (LEO *is really taken aback. He* glances at the others, awkwardly, *then goes quietly and tentatively to* NORA. *The intro but not the main melody of "Three O'clock in the Morning" is heard*)

LEO

Nora, honey—I'm sorry.
> (*And* he *is*)

I was just trying to help.

NORA
(Avoiding him, swinging chair away)

I don't care what you were trying to do.

LEO
(*Moving around chair to face her*)

Listen, I'll go. I'll go quietly, all by myself. But not till you say I'm forgiven.

(*Extending his hands in supplication*)

NORA

You're not forgiven.

LEO
(*Kneeling beside her*)

Nora. Haven't we always been buddies? Who else would go with you to the car wash because you're afraid to drive through the water by yourself.

(She *turns her head away from him, refusing to answer.* He *touches her shoulder to make her look back*)

Who gets up early on Sunday morning to buy you a *Times* before they're gone?

NORA
(*Grudgingly*)

You do.

LEO

Who brings your books back to the public library?

NORA

Oh, all right, Leo.

LEO

If you forgive me, prove it.

NORA

How?

LEO
(*Rising, tilting his head toward the familiar music*)
Dance with me.

NORA
(*Dismissing the idea*)
Here? Now?
(*Suddenly recognizes the main melody, as does* OLIVER.
They *exchange startled glances across the room*)

LEO
Sure. This is my mother's favorite song. I owe it to her to dance.
(*Extending his hands, grinning*)
Do it for The Gipper! Come on, you'll get to hug me. Admit it!
You've always wanted to hug me!

NORA
(*Giving in, letting him pull her to her feet*)
Oh, you're hopeless, hopeless, hopeless!

LEO
(*To* NORA, *as they start to dance*)
And I'm not much of a dancer, either.

(*The others, who have been thrown by* NORA's *outburst
and tears, watch them dance for a moment, somewhat
relieved. Then, as the music continues,* OLIVER *goes to*
CARRIE)

OLIVER
(*An offer to dance*)
Carrie?

(CARRIE *hesitates, looks about her a bit uncomfortably,
especially at* NORA)

It's not supposed to be a spectator sport.

> (CARRIE *joins him tentatively, but dances perfectly well*)

Ah! You dance a lot!

> (CARRIE *looks up at him, forces a small smile, shakes her head* no)

Carrie silent? I don't believe this.

LEO
> (*Who has been keeping an eye on* CARRIE *and* OLIVER)

Time to change partners.

> (LEO *leaves* NORA *and taps* CARRIE *on the shoulder. Gives* CARRIE *a courtly bow, as at dancing school, and* CARRIE *responds with a curtsey.* CARRIE *moves easily into* LEO's *arms, leaving* NORA *and* OLIVER *somewhat awkwardly stranded, standing slightly apart. Finally* OLIVER *approaches* NORA, *determined to preserve the civilities and doing his best to be casual about it*)

OLIVER
> (*To* NORA)

Shall we?

NORA
> (*Frosty*)

Thank you, no. I'll stand this one out.

OLIVER
Why? Are you afraid that Peter will be jealous?

NORA
No.

OLIVER

Oh, you're afraid Carrie will be.

NORA

Don't be ridiculous.

OLIVER

Then you're afraid of me!

NORA

You flatter yourself.

OLIVER

All the time.
(*Putting his arm around her waist firmly*)
I'm not going to dance with Peter, so you'll just have to tag along.

(OLIVER *carries her along with him.* LEO *and* OLIVER *continue dancing with their partners until* PETER *gets up, taps* CARRIE *on the shoulder, and starts to dance very well with her. The mood is allowed to go on for a few moments until, quite suddenly,* CARRIE *walks quickly to the wall switch and snaps off the music, then turns to the others*)

CARRIE
(*Calmly, firmly*)
Peter, I think we should go home now, okay?

PETER

For good?

CARRIE

For whatever.

OLIVER

Carrie!

PETER
(*Glad to be one up on* OLIVER)

All right.

OLIVER
(*To* CARRIE)

Are you sure you know what you're doing?

CARRIE
(*To* OLIVER)

I was waiting for him to lift one finger to stop me. I'm counting that as one finger. You saw I was strangely quiet here for a while. I was just so *curious!* I was waiting to hear how it would turn out —like it was all happening to somebody else! Oliver, you make things so real. I could see that girl flying off to Paris. And I thought, "Yay! Good for her!" But it wouldn't be good for me. I'm not up to that yet. That's graduate work. Besides, Peter needs me. He needs me to be dissatisfied with. Otherwise, he'd have nothing to yearn for. And that's important to him.
(*To* PETER)

Isn't it?

PETER

I'd have to think about that.

OLIVER

The hell with Peter! What do *you* need?

CARRIE
(*Brightly*)

I don't need anything! I feel as if I finally had my coming-out party! I think I'm going to like it . . . out.

(*Crosses to* OLIVER)

Oliver, thank you. We got what we ordered.

OLIVER

(*With a trace of sadness*)

Yes, we got what we ordered. I do that a lot. I order things without checking the price. Then I'm surprised to see how much they cost.

NORA

It's inflation, Oliver. We're all paying more.

CARRIE

Good night, Mrs. DeVreck. We had a very . . . we had a most unusual time.

(*To herself*)

Now, where's my bag?

(*Spotting the sofa* they *used for their "restaurant date"*)

Oh, I left it in the booth!

NORA

(*Her head snapping around in surprise*)

The booth?

CARRIE

(*A trace flustered by this*)

I mean the sofa, I mean the bench—

(*In passing,* she *sees* LEO's *lottery basket, seizes it, possibly as a diversion*)

Oh!—I want to see. Just for fun.

(*She draws a slip of paper from the basket and reads it*)

It says "Leo."

LEO

And it's not a bad idea.

CARRIE
(*Laughing and running to* LEO *to give him a hug*)
I'm going to keep this forever. To remember you!

LEO
Remember me? I'll be on your doorstep tomorrow to pick up that dress!

(*Meantime* PETER *and* NORA *have drifted toward the front door*)

PETER
(*To* NORA)
You said you wanted more time together. But when it looked like you were going to get it, you panicked, didn't you?

NORA
Something like that.
(*Suddenly*)
Peter, I'm sorry.

PETER
(*Meaning it*)
It's all right.

CARRIE
(*Has moved from* LEO *to* OLIVER, *who is standing by himself feeling pretty thoroughly abandoned*)
Oliver, you really are a wonderful counselor. You've been such a help to me.
(*Very slight pause for thought*)
But I *will* have further adjustments to make and I think I should continue with therapy. Is there another therapist you could recommend?

OLIVER
(*Professionally, taking it at face value*)
Yes, certainly, I could give you the names of a couple of men who—

CARRIE
(*Interrupting*)
Actually, it would be much simpler to continue with you. But I suppose that's out of the question. Your wife wouldn't hear of it—now that she's been made kind of insecure. Just please write down a name for me.

(OLIVER *starts to jot down a memo*)

NORA
(*Bristling*)
My dear, I would not have you shopping around for a therapist because of my "insecurities." I assure you I'll manage just fine.

CARRIE
(*Over her shoulder to* PETER, *who is really looking at* NORA)
What about you, Peter? Do *you* think I should find a new therapist?

PETER
I think all therapy is a waste of time. But suit yourself.

CARRIE
(*Turning full to* OLIVER)
Well, then. Can you fit me in next week?

OLIVER
(*It's beginning to dawn on him. He reaches for his appointment book*)
Well—I'll see.

(*Gaining confidence*)
What time of day did you have in mind?

CARRIE

Oh, any afternoon.

OLIVER
(*The plunge, as* he *studies the book*)
No-o-o-o, the afternoons seem to be gone.
                (*As innocently as* he *can manage*)
What about the hour before lunch?

CARRIE
(*Pondering*)

Twelve to one?

OLIVER
(*Repeating it quickly, almost overlapping*)
Twelve to one.

CARRIE
(*As both nod*)

Sure. What day?

OLIVER

Tuesday?

CARRIE

Tuesday. Fine! Well, good night.
                (*To* PETER, *smiling, but it* is *a command*)
Come on, Peter.

(CARRIE *and* PETER *leave*)

OLIVER
(*Big sigh, concealing any trace of exhilaration* he *may feel*)
Well! Finally!

LEO
Let's do this every Saturday night!

(NORA *is picking up some glasses and* LEO's *lottery basket*. She *takes them to the kitchen*)

Ask yourself. What would you have done without me today?

OLIVER
(*Shaking his head ruefully*)
Oh, Leo, the eggs I broke . . . to make this omelet.

(NORA *bursts in from the kitchen, holding* LEO's *lottery basket*)

NORA
Leo! You are an absolute, total idiot!

LEO
Is that all? I thought you had news.

NORA
(*To* OLIVER)
Do you know that all three slips in this basket said "Leo"?

LEO
I *have* to try harder. I'm lonesome.
(LEO *gives a little wave and disappears onto the deck, flicking the music switch on again so that "Three O'clock in the Morning" resumes*)

OLIVER
(*Indicating the music*)

Our social director is still at work.

NORA

I hear.

OLIVER
(*Extending his arms for a dance*)

I guess it's required.

> (NORA *slips into his arms more confidently now, and*
> they *dance a few bars before* she *speaks. As* she *speaks,*
> they *stop dancing but keep their arms casually about*
> *each other as* they *drift downstage, strolling in rhythm,*
> *facing front*)

NORA

Oliver, when you pretended to call your secretary earlier to make the plane reservations, what number did you call?

OLIVER

I don't understand.

NORA

Well, you didn't call your secretary. But you dialed *some* number. Was it the weather?

OLIVER
(*Sagely*)

Oh—you figured that out.

NORA
(*Complacently*)

Sure. The whole business was just a big act to keep me here. You can't fool me.

OLIVER
(*Smiling as he stands back to look at her, holding both her hands*)
Honey, I *knew* I could never fool you.
(*And now he sweeps her into great dance swirls about the room, thinking his own private thoughts and grinning like a fool*)

(*Music up full for:*)

CURTAIN